SURVIVING PROCEDURES
AFTER A SEXUAL ASSAULT

THIRD EDITION

Surviving Procedures After A Sexual Assault

THIRD EDITION

by

Megan Ellis

press gang publishers

*This publication is intended as general legal information only
and should not form the basis of legal advice of any kind.*

Canadian Cataloguing in Publication Data
Ellis Megan, 1955–
   Surviving procedures after a sexual assault
ISBN 0-88974-011-9
   1. Rape—Canada.   2. Trials (Rape)—Canada.
3. Rape Victims—Services for—Canada.
I. Title.
HV6569.C2E44 1988   362.8'83'0971   C88-091003-8

Originally published by Women Against Violence Against Women/Rape
Crisis Centre, 1985. Funds for the original edition provided by the
Legal Services Society and the Law Foundation of British Columbia.

Type produced by Baseline Type & Graphics Cooperative
Edited and designed by Penny Goldsmith
Graphics by Claire Kujundzic
Layout by Val Speidel

First printing of third edition: January 1988
Second printing: September 1989
Printed by the collective labour of Press Gang Printers
Printed and bound in Canada

Press Gang Publishers
603 Powell Street,
Vancouver, B.C. V6A 1H2

Acknowledgements

This book was produced with the help of the following people and organizations:

• Deborah Bradley and Stephanie Crate of WAVAW/Rape Crisis Centre in Vancouver, whose comments and support during the writing of the first draft are greatly appreciated;

• Barbara Field of the Victoria Women's Sexual Assault Centre, Jan Forde of WAVAW/Rape Crisis Centre, Vancouver, Sally-Anne Garrett-Rempel of the Terrace Sexual Assault Centre, Professor Lynn Smith of the University of British Columbia, Faculty of Law, and Georgia Williams, all of whom read the manuscript and provided many valuable comments and suggestions;

• Wendy Harvey, Crown Counsel, for her assistance with changes to the second and third editions;

• Pat Marshall and Kate Andrew of the (Toronto) Metro Action Committee on Public Violence Against Women and Children, who provided information and encouragement for the second edition;

• many others, too numerous to list, who read and provided help with various sections of the book;

• members of the WAVAW/Rape Crisis Centre collective in Vancouver who provided encouragement and carried on with the work; and

• Penelope Goldsmith, who edited her way through stacks of returned drafts, who provided crucial assistance at every stage, and whose patience and commitment were essential throughout.

Any errors and opinions expressed are my own.

And I thank all the women. . . who survive, who work, who learn, who teach, who fight to change.

Table of Concordance

From time to time Parliament consolidates and re-organizes the federal statutes. As a consolidation is currently underway, most section numbers of the Criminal Code have been changed. The numbers in this book are the old section numbers; the new numbers are listed in the following table. Please consult this list in reference to Appendix I.

Old Section Number (R.S.C. 1970, c. C-34)	Revised Number (R.S.C. 1985, c. C-46)
122	133
124	136
127	139
139	150.1 (projected)
140	151
141	152
146	153
150	155
154	159
155	160
166	170
167	171
168	172
169	173
170	174
173	177
195	212
244	265
245	266
245.1	267
245.2	268
245.3	269
246.1	271
246.2	272
246.3	273
246.4	274
246.5	275
246.6	276
246.7	277
246.8	278
247	279
330	372
442	486
455	504
688	753
745	810

Table Of Contents

Introduction **15**

The Law And Sexual Violence **18**
   The Criminal Law   18
   History Of Rape Law   18
   1983 Changes To The Sexual Assault Law   19
   1988 Changes To The Sexual Assault Law   21

Reporting A Sexual Assault **22**
   Children—The Legal Duty To Report   22
   Adults—The Decision   22
   Medical Information   24
   If You Don't Want To Report   24
   Make A Third Party Report   25
   If You Have Decided To Report   26

Special Procedures For Young Victims **27**
   Laws To Protect Children And Young People   27
   Special Procedures   28
   The Duty To Report   29
   The Investigation   29
   Sexual Abuse In The Home   29
   Criminal Procedures   30
   The Court Process   31
   Adult Survivors Of Child Sexual Abuse   32
   Sentencing   32

The Police Investigation **33**
   The Role Of The Police   33
   The Medical Examination   34
   After The Medical Examination   35
   The Interview   35
   Your Statement   36
   Police Questioning   37
   The Polygraph   38

Procedures To Identify The Attacker **40**
   Going To A Police Line-up   40
   Hypnosis   41

For Your Protection **42**
    Police Protection 42
    Peace Bonds 43
    Protecting Yourself 43

Laying Charges **45**
    Kinds Of Sexual Assault Charges 45
    The Decision To Lay Charges 46
    What You Can Do If No Charges Are Laid 47
    Laying An Information Before A Justice Of The Peace 48
    Trying To Get The Charges Dropped 49
    Staying Charges 50
    Plea Bargaining 50

Types Of Offences **52**
    Indictable Offences 52
    Summary Offences 52
    Summary Procedures 52
    Sexual Offences 53

Young Offenders **54**

The Arrest **56**

Bail **58**
    The Bail Hearing 58
    Release With Conditions 59
    No-contact Provision 60
    Changing Bail Conditions 60
    Breaking Conditions Of Bail 60

Getting Information About Your Case **62**

Waiting For The Next Step **63**
    Remembering Details 63
    Change Of Address 64
    If You Change Your Mind 64

Interview With Crown Counsel **65**
    The Role Of Crown Counsel 65
    Having Your Own Representative 65
    Before The Interview With Crown Counsel 66
    The Interview 67
    Special Procedures 68

Election By The Accused **69**
    More Than One Accused 69
    Changing An Election 70

Courtroom Personnel **71**
    The Judge 71
    The Crown Counsel 71
    The Defence Counsel 71
    The Court Clerk 72
    The Court Stenographer 72
    The Sheriffs 72
    The Jury 72

Information On Being A Witness **75**
    Being Called As A Witness 76
    Before You Are Called To Testify 76
    Your Testimony 77
    Identifying The Attacker 78
    Cross-Examination 79
    Self-Incrimination 79
    Perjury 80
    After Testifying 80
    Witness Fees 81

Media Coverage **82**
    Request By The Accused For A Ban On Publication 82
    Request By The Victim For A Ban On Publication 83
    Talking To The Media 83

Special Rules Of Evidence For Sexual Offences **85**
    The Issue Of Consent 85
    Recent Complaint 87
    Past Sexual History 88
    Corroboration 89
    Similar Fact Evidence 90

The Preliminary Hearing **92**
    Moving The Hearing 93
    Excluding The Public 93
    Mentally Ill Accused 94
    The Hearing 94
    Appeal From A Decision On A Preliminary Hearing 95
    Transcripts 95

The Trial **97**
    Pre-Trial Motions 97
    Arraignment—The Accused Pleads 98
    Mentally Ill Accused 99
    Adjournments 99
    Motion For Mistrial 99

The Case For The Crown 100
Voir Dire 101
Cross-Examination By Defence Counsel 102
Motion To Dismiss 103
The Case For The Defence 103
Available Defences 103
Closing Statements By Counsel 104
The Judge's Charge To The Jury 104
The Verdict 105

Sentencing **107**
The Concept Of Sentencing 107
Sentencing Considerations 107
Victim Impact Statements 108
Sentencing Procedure 109
Sentencing Options 109
Dangerous Offenders 111

Appeals **112**
Appeal Procedure 112

Criminal Injury Compensation **114**
To Apply For Criminal Injury Compensation 115
Interim Payments 116
Medical Information 117
Where The Decision Is Made By An Adjudicator 117
If You Do Not Agree With The Adjudicator's Decision 118
Where A Hearing Is Held 118
If You Receive An Award 119

Suing Your Attacker **120**

Sexual Harassment At Work **122**
Human Rights Complaint 122
Trade Union Protection 123
Unfair Dismissal 123

Appendix I – The Criminal Code – Sexual Offences **125**

Appendix II – The Polygraph Test **134**

Suggested Reading **136**

Personal Record **139**

Preface to the Third Edition

The federal government has recently made important changes to the Criminal Code concerning sexual offences against children and young people. These new amendments abolish a number of old offences such as sexual intercourse with girls under age fourteen, and between the ages of fourteen and sixteen of "previously chaste character", and introduce several new offences including "sexual interference" and "sexual exploitation". In addition, they include various provisions which are aimed at making the legal procedures somewhat less difficult for young victims.

These changes are a long overdue response to the growing awareness of sexual abuse and its consequences. They are a direct result of survivors of child sexual abuse, now grown women, speaking out about their experience. More recently many more children and young people have themselves begun to tell about what is happening to them. This new law recognizes that children have a right to be listened to and believed.

The new procedures are included in the sections of the book to which they relate, and the new offences are listed in Appendix I. As the amendments have only just been made law, it is not possible to predict exactly what effects they will have. Certainly procedures will continue to vary from region to region; their effectiveness will depend upon the willingness of governments and of individual police, crown counsel and judges to carry out their work with the understanding that the new law requires and that children and young people deserve.

Megan Ellis
January, 1988

Introduction

This handbook was written to be used by anyone across Canada who has survived a sexual assault or who wants to know more about the procedures after a sexual assault. It was put together by a rape crisis centre worker who has gone through the medical, police and court procedures with many survivors of sexual assault. The experiences of these women, their concerns, fears, questions and opinions have formed the basis of this book.

Although every sexual assault survivor is different and every case is different, many of the concerns and questions that women have are similar. This manual is a result of what has been learned by these women and by the rape crisis centres which they have contacted.

The procedures that a survivor may go through after a sexual assault are often difficult and confusing. This book explains these procedures so that you will understand the different things you can do as well as the different kinds of help the medical, police and legal workers might offer to you or expect from you.

Procedures may vary somewhat from province to province, but this book will give you the basic information about what will happen after the assault. You can get help in your area from a rape crisis centre or other community organizations.

While it is true that some boys and men are victims of sexual assault, and a very few women commit sexual assault, sexual violence is primarily an act of violence committed by men against women and female children. Sexual assault is very much related to the power differences between men and women in society; it is one of the ways men maintain their power over women. For this reason the handbook refers to the person committing the sexual assault as "he" and to the person who has been sexually assaulted as "she".

Being the victim of a rape or any form of sexual violence is a terrible and difficult experience. Sexual assault is an act of violence. Men commit sexual assault in order to feel powerful. By making someone feel humiliated and degraded they get a feeling of control.

Being the victim of a sexual assault means having your power taken away. Sexual assault is always a life-threatening situation. During a sexual assault you do not know if you are going to be injured or even killed. You are aware that you have no control over what is going to happen to you. You know that the attacker doesn't care about what you want, he just cares about getting what he wants—power and control.

Each woman recovers from a sexual assault differently. It often takes quite a while to get back the feeling of having control over your own life. Sometimes the complicated medical and legal procedures make you feel even more confused. Sometimes police or legal workers do not take the time to explain the different steps of the investigation or procedures. Lack of information about all these things can make you feel even more powerless. You might think that while everyone is talking about what happened to you, nobody is really telling you what's going on, and nobody is asking you what you think.

Sometimes the different workers who you deal with will try to explain things to you. They may use words or phrases that you do not understand. You may not feel that you want to take up more of their time to get them to explain more clearly. You may feel that they expect you to know about the words they are using.

This handbook will help to make the medical and legal procedures less confusing, but having it doesn't mean that you can't ask questions. You have a right to know what is going on. While this handbook will explain many of the different steps in a sexual assault case, there may be special things about your case that you will want to ask the police, the prosecutor or a rape crisis centre worker about.

You are the person who was attacked. You are also a member of the public. For these two reasons you have a right to know about your case and you have a right to question the way that it is being handled. This handbook will be helpful in figuring out the kinds of questions you may want to ask, and which workers may be able to give you the information you need.

It may be useful to use the handbook as a guidebook to a strange and complicated system. It will give you information about the players and the rules of the game. It will not tell you what moves to make. It will help you to figure out what you need to know and how to find out the information to make your own decisions. You might find it helpful to ask a friend to read this handbook with you, so you can talk about the decisions you need to make.

This handbook was written to try to help you get back some of the power that was taken away from you by the sexual assault. Many women who have gone through the procedures after a sexual assault have said that those procedures made them feel powerless and afraid all over again.

Knowing more about what your rights are, about the different choices you can make, and about how the legal system works is a way of becoming stronger and fighting back. Talking with other women and learning from their experiences is also a way to feel that you are not alone.

Many women, sexual assault survivors, have gone through the court system to try and make sure that justice is done. Some of them have become more bitter, some of them have felt silenced, but some of them have continued to speak out so that other women will know. It is their hope and our hope that the voices of survivors will provide the fuel for the work which will one day make violence against women unthinkable and impossible.

It is to all these women that this handbook is dedicated.

The Law and Sexual Violence

The Criminal Law

Criminal laws are laws which define the kinds of things which individuals are not allowed to do. They are laws which the government makes in order to protect the kind of society we have now from people who do things which are harmful or disruptive. The criminal law is a kind of social code. It defines what behaviour is unacceptable. The kinds of things which are not acceptable change over the years and are different in different societies.

Most crimes, including the different forms of sexual violence, are listed in the Criminal Code of Canada. The Criminal Code defines the different offences, the penalties for committing those offences and the procedures for dealing with the people who are accused of committing them.

Judges have the important role of deciding how a general definition in the Criminal Code will be applied to particular situations. How judges interpret the law and what they have said about it in other cases (called precedents) is used to clarify how the law will be applied in your case. In order to have an idea of how a section of the Criminal Code will be used it is useful to find out about how judges have used it in past cases.

History Of Rape Law

Rape was originally seen as a crime of theft of sexual property. A rapist would often have to pay money in damages to the woman's husband or father, because the woman was seen as having lost her value as a marriageable daughter or as a pure wife.

A woman who was raped was supposed to run and tell people right away to prove that she was not at fault. Few people understood that it was very hard for women to talk about being raped. A man who forced his wife to have sexual intercourse could not be charged with rape, because husbands were supposed to be able to have sex with their wives whenever they wanted.

A lot of myths developed about rape. Many people believed that if a woman got raped it was her own fault. They thought that only certain kinds of women got raped. These attitudes meant that women who were raped did not want to tell people because they were afraid of being blamed. Because women did not tell, many people thought that rape did not happen very often.

Often when women did report their rape, people seemed to suspect that they had done something to provoke the rapist. Sometimes they were not believed. Rape was explained by saying that it was women's fault.

These attitudes were also common among people who worked in the criminal justice system. A study done in Vancouver (Clark, Lorenne; Lewis, Debra "A Study of Rape in Canada: Phases "C" and "D", *Report to the Donner Foundation*, 1976, unpublished) found that of the 378 rapes reported to the police from 1970-1974 only 54 cases went to trial, and only 27 of these resulted in the attacker being found guilty. The authors of this study estimated that only one in four rapes was reported to the police and that therefore only 1.8% of all rapes resulted in a conviction. They found that how the police dealt with the case had more to do with the character and background of the victim than with the rape or the rapist.

The treatment of rape cases in the courts also reflected many of these attitudes. Women were often questioned about their past sexual history because it was thought that this related to whether or not they were telling the truth. If a woman had not reported the rape right away it was sometimes suggested that she had used the time to make up some or all of the story. Judges had to warn juries that rape victims were not reliable witnesses.

1983 Changes To The Sexual Assault Law

The parts of the Criminal Code which relate to sexual violence against adults were changed in January, 1983. These changes were made by Parliament after rape crisis centres, women's groups and many others continued ten years of protest against the way rape victims were treated by the courts. However, the lawmakers did not adopt all the recommendations put forward by feminists, but settled on a compromise, leaving a number of important problems basically unchanged.

The discussion about the issue of rape and the treatment of rape victims has been part of an important change in the way many people view rape. More people now understand that rape, or sexual assault, is an act of violence, that no woman wants to be raped. They are aware that most women are raped by someone who they know. They have heard that the only thing which rape victims have in common, other than the fact that they are almost all female, is that they were vulnerable. While the old views are still held by many, including many people who work in the criminal justice system, these changes in attitudes sometimes have an important effect on how women who are survivors of sexual assault will be treated.

The new law contains several important differences. The old crime of rape was removed and three types of sexual assault were created. The names of the offences were changed because it was thought that the label 'sexual assault' more accurately reflected the violent nature of the crimes. The new offences of sexual assault were intended to cover all kinds of unwanted sexual touching from bottom-pinching to attacks which include forced sexual intercourse (still commonly called rape) and the use of a weapon or wounding.

Changes to the special court procedures used in rape cases were also made. There was some attempt to restrict the kinds of questions a defence lawyer could ask about a victim's past sexual activity and to prevent the defence from using information about a woman's sexual reputation to suggest that she is not telling the truth.

However, the interpretations of the new law by the courts have been a serious disappointment to those concerned about protections for victims of sexual violence. Men accused of sexual offences have used the Charter of Rights and Freedoms to argue that the procedural protections in the sexual assault law interfere with their right to a fair trial. Others have argued that special protections for young women were discriminatory on the basis of age or sex. Some judges have defined 'sexual assault' in a way which does not include many kinds of offensive touching. And sentences for those convicted of sexual offences often do not reflect the seriousness with which many women view the crime.

In addition, the fact that all the offences are worded in 'gender-neutral' terms serves to hide the reality that it is almost always men who sexually assault, and usually women who are sexually assaulted. This 'gender blindness' is used to deny women the special protections they need precisely because of the sexist attitudes to victims of sexual violence in particular and to women in general. Unfortunately, the 'liberty' and 'equality' guaranteed by the Charter is being used to try to undermine the equal right of women to live free from the fear of sexual violence.

1988 Changes To The Sexual Assault Law

In 1988, Parliament changed the parts of the Criminal Code which deal with sexual offences against children and young people. These new offences are also 'gender-neutral'; they apply equally to boys and girls.

Three new offences—"sexual interference", "invitation to sexual touching" and "sexual exploitation"—were created to protect children and young people from sexual abuse. In addition, the laws of evidence were changed to remove some of the difficulties in getting the stories of children and young people before the courts. Certainly these changes will help children and young people to be heard; we will have to wait to see whether the people in the criminal justice system listen to what they say.

It is important to understand that where someone committed the offence before the laws were changed, they will be charged under the law as it was at the time the offence was committed, not at the time they are charged or at the time of their trial.

The sections of the current Criminal Code which relate to sexual offences are listed at the back of this book in Appendix I. Remember that the offences listed in the Criminal Code are outlines, and that each case may affect and may be affected by how the judge decides to apply the law.

Reporting a Sexual Assault

Children – The Legal Duty To Report

Anyone who has reason to believe that a child under the age of nineteen is in need of protection, that her or his physical or emotional health is threatened, *must* report the situation to the police or to the organization which is responsible for child protection, for example the Ministry of Social Services, Children's Aid Society or Child and Family Services.

Adults – The Decision

As an adult you have no legal obligation to report that you have been the victim of a sexual assault. Probably only one out of every ten women who is sexually assaulted reports the crime to the police.

If you do report the crime to the police, the decision about whether or not charges will be laid against the attacker will not be yours. Either the crown counsel or the police will decide whether there is enough evidence to lay charges.

Women have different reasons for reporting a sexual assault to the police. Sometimes their main concern is to try to make sure that the attacker is imprisoned so that he cannot attack any other women. Sometimes they are afraid that he will come back and assault them again. Sometimes someone else called the police. Or perhaps the woman herself called the police for help right after it happened.

Sometimes women just want to make sure he doesn't get away with it. They may be very angry. They may want to speak out about what happened to them so that other women know that it can and does happen.

All of these are common reasons why women report their sexual assault to the police.

There are also many different reasons why women do not report to the police. Women are often reluctant to tell anyone that they have been sexually assaulted. They may fear that people will think that what happened was their fault. They might be concerned that people will treat them differently or gossip about them. They may be too embarrassed to have their family or friends know.

Women are often told by the men who attack them that if they tell anyone he will come back and kill them or rape them again, so sometimes they are afraid to tell anyone about the assault.

Sometimes women have heard about the problems of other women who have had to go to court to talk about their sexual assault. They have heard that the procedures take a long time. They have heard that they will be asked a lot of personal questions. They may know that only a small percentage of the sexual assaults which are reported to the police end up with the attacker being sent to prison. Or they may think that sentences for sexual offenders are so low that it is not worth all the trouble.

They may just want to try and get over what happened to them by themselves or with the help of family, friends or the rape crisis centre. They may think that the best way to cope is to try and forget it all as soon as possible. They fear that the hearing and trial months later will just force them to have to relive the whole experience again.

If you have not yet decided whether to report your sexual assault you may find that reading through some or all of this book will give you more information in order to make your decision. You might want to talk about this information with a friend or a rape crisis worker.

If you are not sure whether you want to report, you should write down or tape record what you remember about what happened to you. Include as much detail as possible. This is a way of making sure you don't forget things during the time it takes to make your decision.

A written or recorded statement will be helpful if you later decide to report to the police. Getting someone you know to witness that you have written or recorded a statement will help to show that the information was recorded quite soon after the sexual assault.

Medical Information

Whether or not you want to report the rape to the police, *it is very important to get a doctor to give you a checkup.* You may not have any injuries that you can see, but you should get checked just in case. Your own doctor or a hospital emergency room will do this for you. They will also check for VD and should offer you treatment to prevent a possible pregnancy.

If you would prefer to be examined by a woman doctor you can ask whether there is one available. Shaughnessy Hospital in Vancouver has specially trained women doctors on call during the day and night. Some other hospitals will provide a woman doctor if you ask.

Most hospitals will not call the police in if you do not want them involved. Some hospitals will give you a medical examination and keep any evidence they find until you have made up your mind about whether you want to report. You can phone the nearest rape crisis centre or you can call the hospital before going there to find out what their policy is. If you want, you can ask a friend, family member or rape crisis centre worker to go with you.

If You Don't Want To Report

Deciding not to report your sexual assault to the police doesn't mean that you have to cope with it on your own. Here are some things you might want to do:

Talk to Friends and Family

You can talk to your friends and family about it. Their sympathy and support may be very helpful to you at this time.

See a Doctor

You should see a doctor for a medical examination.

Call a Rape Crisis or Sexual Assault Centre

You can call up a rape crisis or sexual assault centre. (Rape crisis centres and sexual assault centres are different names for what is generally the same service.) Most of these centres have 24-hour lines, so that you can talk to them when you want. They are often listed in the inside front cover of the telephone book or under "R" or "S" in the phone book.

You will not have to give your name if you don't want to. They will not tell anyone else about what you have told them. Rape crisis/sexual assault centres have trained women on call who will provide counselling, support and information. You can also get their help to deal with your friends or family members if they are having difficulty coping with what has happened, or don't understand the real nature of sexual assault.

Make A Third Party Report

You can pass on information about the sexual assault and the attacker to the police, without letting them know who you are. This is called a **third party report**. To make a third party report you give the information about what happened, plus a description of the attacker to a rape crisis worker. She writes it up on a form and gives it to the police. The form does not have any information about who you are on it. The police will not know your identity, but they will then know about your attacker.

They cannot use the third party report to arrest him or take him to court, but they will have the information about who he is and what he has done. This means that if he attacks someone else they will have some background information on him and may be able to find him more easily.

If he did attack someone else in the same way that he attacked you, the police might want to speak to you to get more information. Then they would contact the rape crisis centre worker who had sent in the form and ask her to contact you. She would phone you and ask you if you wanted to give more information to the police. If you said yes she would go with you to talk with them. If you said no she would tell the police that you didn't want to talk with them and she would not give them any more information about you or about what you had told her. Most rape crisis centres will do their utmost to keep your identity confidential.

Make a Human Rights Complaint

If your attack happened in your place of work you might want to make a complaint to the Human Rights Commission. (See the section on *Sexual Harassment at Work* for procedures.)

Confrontation

If the man who attacked you is someone you know, you might want to think of ways that you could let him know directly what you think about what he did. Or you might want a way to tell people that he knows about what he did. You can talk to your friends or to a rape crisis centre about ways to do this.

Criminal Injury Compensation

You may be able to apply for financial compensation for your injuries or losses. The procedures are explained in the section on Criminal Injury Compensation.

Civil Suit for Damages

You can get advice about suing your attacker in a civil court (see the section *Suing Your Attacker*).

If You Have Decided To Report

If you want to report your sexual assault to the police, it is important to report as soon as possible. Delay might mean that evidence is lost or destroyed. The police will also want you to tell them about what happened while all the details are still fresh in your mind.

You may really want to wash or shower. However, having a bath, changing your clothes, combing your hair or even brushing your teeth might destroy important evidence of what happened. If you can, wait until after the medical examination before washing or going to the washroom.

You do not have to call the police before you go for the medical examination. You can go to the hospital right away and ask someone at the hospital to contact the police or you can call the police and ask them to come and take you to the hospital.

You can ask for a friend, family member or rape crisis centre worker to go with you to the hospital and to be with you through the police investigation. You might want to call them first to be sure they will be there when the police arrive.

Special Procedures for Young Victims

Some studies estimate that as many as one-half of all girls and one-third of all boys, under the age of eighteen have been sexually abused (*Sexual Offences Against Children*, Report of the Committee on Sexual Offences Against Children and Youths, Ottawa, 1984). The abusers are almost all male.

Like adult women who have been victims of rape, children have traditionally been afraid to tell anyone, or when they have told they have often not been believed. Sometimes children who have been sexually abused, act out or misbehave as a way of expressing their fears or pain. These children are sometimes classed as 'problem' or 'bad' children, an attitude which is used as an excuse for not believing them. However, many studies have shown that children do not lie about being sexually abused.

The courts will not admit the testimony of expert witnesses, such as psychologists, to talk about studies which show that children do not lie about being sexually abused. However, the courts are beginning to allow experts to give evidence on ways that a child's behaviour can be an indication that the child has been a victim of sexual abuse.

Laws To Protect Children And Young People

There are special sections in the Criminal Code which are aimed at protecting children from sexual abuse. These sections were updated in 1988. While all of the normal sexual assault offences apply to children, there are additional special offences which relate to the sexual abuse of children and young people because they are seen as being in need of extra protection.

For example, a man may be charged with touching for a sexual purpose, or having sexual relations with, a girl under the age of fourteen. He may say that she consented, but this is not a legal excuse. It is also not an excuse if he says he didn't know she was under the age of fourteen unless he took all reasonable steps to find out her age.

It is also an offence for a person in a position of trust or authority over someone between the ages of fourteen and eighteen to engage in any sexual activity with them.

These laws reflect an understanding that children and young people are sometimes persuaded or pressured by adults to do things that they don't want to do. In these situations the adult often does not have to use threats or force; the age difference, or the authority of the adult will sometimes be enough to get the child to submit.

In addition, while it is a general rule that wives and husbands cannot be forced to testify against each other, this protection does not apply in cases of sexual assault or child abuse where a spouse is a witness to the activity.

The special laws are, however, very difficult to apply because of the particular problems that are involved in cases of child sexual abuse.

Special Procedures

The criminal justice system, after years of pressure from people who work with children and/or sexual assault victims, has only just begun to try to develop special procedures for dealing with the sexual abuse of children.

The quality of treatment that sexually abused children get varies from place to place. Few social workers and even fewer police officers have any special training in investigating these cases, and there are very few community resources for supporting these children and the people close to them.

Many procedures have been suggested, and a few are now being tested. The wide variety of practices in these cases and the issues around the rights of these children is unfortunately beyond the scope of this handbook. It is our hope that as more children disclose their abuse, and as more adults who have been abused as children speak out, the demands for justice for young victims will provoke much needed change.

The following is a brief summary of some of the general procedures.

The Duty To Report

Any person who has reason to believe that a child (usually someone under nineteen years old) is in need of protection must report the circumstances to the police or to the organization which is responsible for child protection, for example the Ministry of Social Services, Children's Aid Society, or Child and Family Services. Failing to report means that you are committing an offence. Even if you are not sure of the details, you can report. You cannot be charged if the offence cannot be proven as long as you believed the information you gave was true.

The Investigation

Cases are usually first reported to the organizations which are responsible for child protection. The social workers must then notify the police. This means that there will be two sets of investigators in the case. The role of the social workers is to focus on the protection of the child, and the police conduct the criminal investigation.

Where there is reason to suspect that a child is being abused, a social worker should arrange to interview the child. If the abuse involves a family member and was reported by a non-family member this is sometimes done by making contact with the child at school.

Generally the child will be interviewed by a police officer and a social worker together. In some provinces this interview will be videotaped. Making a videotape of the interview has two purposes: it reduces the number of times that a child has to tell the story, and if it is made not too long after the offence was committed it may be used in court in addition to the child's testimony. Sometimes the interviewers will use 'anatomically correct' dolls (dolls which have genitals) to assist the child to describe what has happened. In order to try to assess whether the child has been sexually assaulted the social worker may also arrange for a doctor to do a medical examination.

Sexual Abuse In The Home

Where a child is being sexually abused by a father, step-father, or other relative in their own home, and the offender is arrested and charged, the police or crown counsel should auto-matically request that a condition of his release (bail) be that he have no contact with the child. A judge can impose this order even where it means that the offender will have to move out of his own home.

Where the offender has not been charged, social workers will sometimes manage to convince the abuser to leave the home. Sometimes the mother of the abused child will decide to leave the home. She can move out and then may get a peace bond or restraining order which is an order of the Family or Supreme Court saying that the offender cannot contact the child or herself. She will need legal help to get a restraining order. Legal aid will usually be available for this kind of situation.

The mother can apply for a peace bond at Family Court by swearing an Information saying that she fears the man will cause personal injury to her child. In order to grant the peace bond the judge must be convinced of the danger to the child. (See *For Your Protection*.)

Where the parents are not willing to separate during the investigation, the social worker may decide to remove the child from the home and to place her/him in a foster home. This may seem unfair as it can have the effect of making the child feel like s/he is being punished, but social workers have a duty to protect the child.

If the social workers decide that it is necessary to remove the child from the home they must apprehend the child, which means taking her or him into the care of the Ministry or Child-ren's Aid Society. After they apprehend they must, within seven days, explain their decision to a judge in the Family Court. The parents of the child will be at the hearing and can argue against the apprehension.

Criminal Procedures

If charges are laid, the child will be interviewed a number of times by the crown counsel. In some provinces crown counsel have developed special procedures for dealing with cases of child sexual abuse. These include assigning one crown counsel to oversee all child sexual abuse cases, trying to make sure that the crown counsel assigned to the case is involved from the beginning and stays with the case all the way through to the end of the trial, and increasing the liaison between the crown counsel and the other people who are working with the child, including doctors, social workers and counsellors.

As yet, few crown counsel have received training in dealing with cases of child sexual abuse. There are still some crown counsel who may be reluctant to believe the child. Some may be hesitant to take the case to trial because of concern that a jury will not believe the child or that the child will not be able to cope with the trial process.

The Court Process

As is explained in the section on *Media Coverage*, a victim of a sexual offence can ask the judge at the preliminary hearing or trial to make an order to prevent the media from publishing her name or any information which might reveal her identity. This also applies to a witness in a sexual offence case who is under the age of eighteen.

The recent amendments to the Criminal Code also allow the judge to let a victim in a sexual offence case, who is under the age of eighteen, testify outside the courtroom or behind a screen so that s/he does not have to see her attacker when s/he is telling the court what happened. The judge will only permit this where the judge thinks it is necessary in order to get the child or young person to tell everything that happened. Also, this is only allowed where the court has the facilities which would make it possible for the judge and/or the jury to watch the child testify, either through closed circuit television or some other arrangement.

Young people over the age of fourteen can be sworn in as witnesses and give testimony in the same way as adults. The judge must decide whether someone under the age of fourteen understands what it means to take the oath and, whether s/he is able to communicate the evidence. Children as young as six have given evidence under oath.

A child who cannot take the oath but is able to communicate the evidence can still give testimony if s/he promises to tell the truth.

As in other criminal cases the prosecution must prove, beyond a reasonable doubt, that the accused is guilty of the offence.

Adult Survivors Of Child Sexual Abuse

Someone who is now an adult, but has been a victim of sexual abuse in the past can choose to report to the police. There is no time limit on reporting, but if charges are laid the trial must take place within a reasonable time after the charge has been laid.

The crown counsel will look over the evidence and decide whether charges will be laid. If the abuse has taken place some time ago, there will probably be difficulty in getting other evidence to help prove what happened. While there is no rule that the testimony of victims of sexual offences be corroborated in order to convict the accused, in practice the courts are very reluctant to convict in cases where the only evidence is the testimony of the victim, particularly where the trial takes place a long time after the offence took place. The testimony of a therapist may be useful in these cases.

Sentencing

Sometimes the abuser will plead guilty to the offence and offer to go into counselling. Sometimes they say that they will plead guilty in order to avoid putting the child through the difficulty of testifying in court.

As yet there are no methods of counselling which have been proven to be effective for the men who sexually assault or abuse children. If they continue to have access to the child many abusers will continue to abuse even while they are in therapy.

The Police Investigation

The Role Of The Police

The police who investigate the sexual assault are the police who cover the area where the crime took place. This may be a local police force or an R.C.M.P. detachment. It is the job of the police to gather the information about what happened; to collect the evidence.

In some provinces, for example Ontario and Manitoba, they will also make decisions about whether there is enough evidence to lay charges. In other provinces, for example British Columbia and Newfoundland, it is the crown counsel who decides whether there is enough evidence to take a case to court.

You can contact the police by calling the emergency number for your area. This number is listed on the inside of the front cover of the telephone book. When you phone to report a sexual assault the radio dispatch will send out a police car to where you are. There may be one or two officers in the car. If you want to have a woman police officer come out to take the information you must ask when you call in. The police will then try to send out a woman officer if there is one available. While waiting for the police to arrive you may want to call a family member, friend or a rape crisis/sexual assault centre.

If you are under sixteen years old your parent or guardian must be told and must give their consent before the police can begin their investigation or before the hospital can treat you, unless it is emergency treatment. If necessary the Ministry of Social Services or Children's Aid can act as a guardian for this purpose.

The officers will listen to your report and make notes. Then they will ask you more specific questions about the time, place, description of the attacker, etc. If you are still in the place where the attack took place they may collect any things which show evidence of what happened.

The Medical Examination

They will then take you to the hospital for the medical examination. This examination will have two purposes: first, to make sure that any injuries you may have are taken care of, and that you get the tests and medications you need. Second, the doctor who examines you will collect any evidence which she or he finds which shows that you have been sexually assaulted. This evidence is called medical-legal evidence or forensic evidence. You will be asked to sign a consent form to have this extra procedure done. Whether or not medical-legal evidence is being collected, the police should *not* be present during your medical examination.

Let the police know if you would prefer to have a woman doctor do the examination. They should then let the hospital know ahead of time. In Vancouver a woman doctor is always present to do sexual assault examinations. Other hospitals will often try to provide a woman doctor if one is available.

The doctor will probably put your clothes in a bag and give them to the police. The police will pass them on to a laboratory who will test them for traces of evidence. You will probably not get them back until after the legal proceedings are over. *Take an extra set of clothes with you to the hospital* or get someone else to bring some clothes for you.

The doctor will examine you carefully. S/he may ask you a bit about your medical history. S/he will also ask you when you last had sexual intercourse in order to be sure that the semen tests will be related to the sexual assault. S/he should also give you a VD test and pills to prevent gonorrhea.

If you did not have birth control and you want to prevent a pregnancy, the doctor should give you hormone pills to make sure that you do not get pregnant. These are hormones known as "morning after" pills and can be used to prevent a pregnancy up to 72 hours after sexual intercourse. The most recommended type of pill is called Ovral. (DES) diethylstilbestrol is sometimes used but is *not* recommended. Be sure to ask the doctor about the possible risks of taking these pills.

The doctor will also write up the medical report and give a copy to the police. You can ask the doctor questions about the medical procedures and about the report.

After The Medical Examination

The hospital examination can take up to an hour, and perhaps longer if the doctor is not able to come immediately. Following the medical examination the police may want to ask you more questions. They may want to call in a police photographer to take pictures of any bruises or other injuries you have. They may even want to take you back to the place where the attack happened to be sure that they find any evidence which might be there before the evidence gets lost or destroyed.

If you do not feel up to answering more questions or to going with them to the place where it happened, tell them. You do not have to go with them. Sometimes police are so concerned to get all the necessary information that they forget that the victim has just been through a very difficult experience. While they may just be trying to do a good investigation, they may need to be reminded that you are tired and need to rest or need to talk to someone who will be supportive; a friend, family member or rape crisis centre worker.

Try to remember to write down the name of the hospital, the name of the doctor you saw and to ask the police officers for their names or badge numbers, or for their business cards. You should also ask for the number that the police will use to identify your case (this is called the case file number) so that later you can find out information about it more easily. At the back of this book is a section called *Personal Record*. You can use it to write down this information.

The police should make sure that someone is taking you home or they should drive you home themselves.

The police may then go to the place where you were attacked and collect any evidence which might show that the assault took place, or any evidence which could be used to identify the attacker. They may also take photographs of the place. They will write up a report to submit to the detectives who will carry on the investigation.

The Interview

The first part of the police investigation will be handled by the police on patrol who are first sent out to answer your call. In most detachments these officers will file their report and then the case will be taken over by officers in plain-clothes. In city and municipal police forces these officers are called detectives. Some police detachments have detectives who specialize in investigating sexual assault cases.

Within a few days after you have reported the officers will contact you to arrange an interview. They may ask you to come into the police station for the interview or, if you wish, one or two may come out to your house. If you want, you can have a friend, family member or rape crisis centre worker with you during this interview.

If you have visible physical injuries, such as bruises, and the police have not yet arranged for your injuries to be photo-graphed, ask the officers whether they will arrange for photo-graphs to be taken.

During the interview you will be asked to tell the whole story again. Everything you say will be written down or tape recorded. As you tell the story you may be asked to be really specific about certain details, especially times, places, in what order things happened, etc.

Although it may be very hard to talk about your experience it is important that you be very clear with the officers about what happened. Do not leave anything out even if you think that it might not be good for your case. If you have trouble answering a question you can ask if you can come back to it later.

When you talk about the parts of the body it is helpful to use the correct names instead of the slang words. Remember that police have heard these kinds of descriptions before and will not be shocked to hear what you say.

Your Statement

After your statement has been written down, read it over very carefully. If there are bits that are not quite right, or are confusing, tell the officers. Make sure that they are changed or made more clear. You will then be asked to sign the statement. Signing it means that you agree that it is a true account of what you said. It is very important that your statement is clear and complete because you will be asked about it if you go to court.

Police Questioning

The police may then ask you questions about your history. If your attacker was someone you know they will ask you questions about your relationship to him. The police will want to know something about you in order to be able to tell what kind of witness you will be if the case goes to court. Their investigation also provides crown counsel with a complete picture of the case so that s/he will be prepared for anything which might come up during a hearing or trial.

Sometimes they will ask you questions which you don't like or which seem very personal. If you object to the questions you can tell them. If you don't understand why they want to know these things you can ask them to explain why they need to know.

You do not have to answer any questions about your past sexual involvement with anyone other than the man who attacked you, or with others who were there when you were attacked. You do not have to answer questions that you object to, although you should be aware that the police can be uncooperative if you refuse to answer their questions.

Sometimes the officers may ask you hard questions because they think it will show whether you will be able to talk about what happened in court, even though in some provinces it is not their decision whether the case goes to court. They can ask the questions, but you have a right to refuse to answer them. You will not be able to refuse to answer questions in court, but in court the judge should ensure that you are only asked questions which relate to the sexual assault.

The police may be angry if you refuse to answer their questions. They may suggest that you are not co-operating with the investigation. You can remind them that you want to help with the investigation but that you won't allow your rights as a person to be violated.

If you feel that the police have treated you unfairly you can call a rape crisis centre for advice on how to deal with the situation. You can also call or write to the chief of police.

If you do not want the police to phone you at your home or at work you should tell the officers. They will probably be willing to contact you or to leave messages for you in a way which will protect your privacy. For example, if you ask them, they will not say that they are police officers when they phone or leave messages.

If you are afraid that your attacker might come back and assault you again you should tell this to the police. They may agree to alert the officers who are patrolling the neighbourhood. If the attacker is picked up they may ask the judge to keep him in custody. If he is released on bail they can request that one of the conditions be that he does not contact you (a no-contact order). They should be aware that you think it is possible that he may come back. You might want to ask if they will provide you with any of the kinds of help listed in the section titled *For Your Protection* of this handbook.

You will probably be contacted again by the detectives. You might be phoned or asked to go in to see them to clarify certain details. Other people who might know something about the attack will probably also be interviewed during this time.

The Polygraph (Lie-Detector Test)

The police might ask you to take a lie-detector test. They sometimes ask women to take the test when the police have other evidence which contradicts some of what the women have said. If you take the lie-detector test and do not pass, the police may stop investigating the case. If the machine shows a positive result that may convince the police to continue their work on the case.

You do not have to take a lie-detector test. The test is *not* reliable. It is used by some police more than others. The results of a lie-detector test cannot be used in court. It sometimes shows that people are telling the truth when they are lying and sometimes shows people as lying when they are really telling the truth. This happens most often when the person taking the test is emotionally upset.

Many rape crisis centres say that women should refuse to take the lie-detector test because it is not a fair test. If you are asked to take the test and you don't want to take it, you can say that you are following the advice of rape crisis centres, and that the information in this booklet shows that it is not reliable. (See *Appendix II* for more detailed information on the polygraph test.)

Procedures to Identify the Attacker

If the attacker was someone who you did not know, it is quite likely that you will be asked to help the police identify him. You will be asked to give the most complete description of him that you can to the police.

Sometimes you will be asked to go down to the police station and look through books of photographs of offenders who are already known to the police.

You may be asked to help them to put together a composite drawing. To make a composite drawing, you are shown several pictures of parts of the face, e.g. chins, eyes, moustaches, etc. You choose the ones that look most like the attacker's. Then a special police artist draws a face using the bits that you have picked out for him. While the drawing that you and the artist come up with will not be exact, it will probably help the police to get a good idea of what the attacker looks like. Doing a composite drawing can take between one and two hours.

Going To A Police Line-up

If the police have someone that they suspect is the attacker they might ask you to come to a line-up. To put together a line-up the police will pick up the suspect and somewhere between five and nine other men who look a bit like him. The suspect will not be told that the line-up is related to his offense.

You will be asked to go down to the police station and to see whether you think that any of the men in the line-up is the man who attacked you. Some rooms used for line-ups have one-way mirrors so that you cannot be seen by the people who are in the line-up. If you think that it will help you to identify him if you hear his voice, you can ask to have all the men say certain words or a phrase.

In cases where the police have a suspect, but cannot find enough men who are similar to the suspect to form a line-up, or do not have the facilities to hold a line-up, the police may bring

Surviving Procedures After A Sexual Assault

you a set of (usually eight) photographs. This set of photographs will include a photo of the suspect. The police will ask if you can pick out your attacker from among the photos.

Hypnosis

Sometimes a witness will not be able to remember even major things about what happened because she was so upset at the time. Hypnosis is sometimes, but rarely, used to help witnesses remember what happened, or to remember what the attacker looked like so that a composite drawing can be done. You will *never* be hypnotised unless you agree to it.

For Your Protection

Many attackers will threaten women after the sexual assault. They say that if you tell the police they will come back and attack you again. While most attackers do not come back you cannot tell which ones will. Most women are afraid of the possibility of being sexually assaulted a second time.

Police Protection

If you have reported the attack to the police, tell them if the attacker threatened to return. Although many police will not offer you protection, there are a few things that the police can do to protect you.

In cases where the police believe that there is a good chance that the attacker may come back and try to kill or injure you they can assist you to relocate to another community. This is called Material Witness Protection. It is used only in cases where the police are convinced that a witness is likely to be in very serious danger from the accused or friends of the accused.

Police will sometimes help a woman who has been sexually assaulted to make contact with a transition house or other community agency which can provide temporary housing. They will sometimes help her and her children to move to a transition house nearby or to one in a different community.

In other cases the police can help by installing an alarm system. They use two different alarm systems. One of them is a kind of a panic button, an alarm you press in your house and which rings at the police station. The other is an intruder alarm system which rings in your house if someone tries to break in.

If you are being harassed over the phone, record the times of all the calls. The police can then be asked to place a tap on the line. They will use this to trace where the call is coming from.

If your attacker has been arrested tell the police you want a no-contact provision as a condition of his bail. If he contacts you, call the police immediately. He can then be re-arrested and a judge will review his bail conditions. If he threatens you and tries to persuade you not to testify against him he can be charged with obstructing justice (Criminal Code subsection 127(3)).

Peace Bonds

If your attacker was your husband or someone you know, and you do not want to press criminal charges against him, you can apply for a peace bond. Under section 745 of the Criminal Code, a person who fears that another person will cause him or her injury, can lay an information before a justice of the peace.

A summons will be issued and a judge will hold a hearing. Both you and the man who attacked you will be present at the hearing.

If the judge agrees that you have reasonable grounds to be afraid of the person s/he will make an order that he must keep the peace. The order will last up to twelve months. The man will not have a criminal record unless he breaches the order, at which point he will be charged.

Protecting Yourself

Whether or not you have reported to the police there are some things you can do to make yourself safer.

You can install your own sturdy locks or alarms. You can get help to figure out ways to make your home safer. You can ask your neighbours to help watch out for you and your home.

Sometimes women who know that the attacker knows where they live decide to move. Moving house is not always practical, and it doesn't seem fair that someone who has been sexually assaulted should also have to move, but if it will make you feel safer it is something you can consider.

Some women decide that they want to carry a weapon or keep one in their homes to defend themselves against any future attack. Weapons are especially dangerous if you don't know how to use them. An attacker can sometimes manage to take a weapon away from you and use it against you. You should consider whether a weapon will increase or decrease your safety.

Learning self-defence is a way that many women have chosen to try to protect themselves. Self-defence courses are often taught as night school programs, by Wen-Do instructors, or by individuals who are specialized in martial arts. Wen-Do is a type of self-defence designed especially for women.

Self-defence is sometimes a good way to help yourself feel stronger and less vulnerable. It is a useful skill and good exercise. Many women find that it is enjoyable and helps them get back a sense of their own power.

Laying Charges

In some provinces it is the police who lay charges, in other provinces, this is the job of crown counsel. You can ask the police or a rape crisis centre worker about who has this responsibility in your province. The crown counsel is a lawyer employed by government to prosecute criminal cases on behalf of society. After the police have finished their initial investigation they, or the crown counsel, will decide whether there is enough evidence to lay a charge against the person who is the suspect. Where the crown counsel lay charges, they will pay a lot of attention to the opinions of the police who did the investigation.

Kinds Of Sexual Assault Charges

The police or crown counsel must also decide which offences in the Criminal Code best fit each case. As listed in Appendix I there are several different sexual offences as well as three different sexual assault offences. There are also two parts of the first kind of sexual assault. These two parts are called 'summary' and 'indictable'. Indictable offences are those which have more serious penalties and which involve more formal procedures. Summary offences carry lower maximum penalties. (See section on *Types of Offences* for a more detailed explanation of these two kinds of offences.)

They will have to decide whether a sexual assault will be treated 'summarily' or 'by way of indictment'. Most sexual assaults will be treated by way of indictment or as 'indictable offences'. Less violent sexual assaults such as minor harassment, bottom-pinching, etc. will be treated summarily. Procedures for summary offences are different than procedures for indictable offences. These procedures are outlined in the next section.

It is important to note that an accused person cannot be convicted of a number of different charges which arise out of the same situation. So while it may appear that there are several sections of the Criminal Code which describe what happened to you, the accused might not be charged with all of them, and he will only be convicted of the most serious charge which is proven beyond a reasonable doubt.

If the police or crown counsel decide to lay charges and to proceed summarily, and you think that the offence should be treated more seriously, ask why the decision was made. If you are not satisfied with the answer, contact a rape crisis centre, or contact a more senior crown counsel. Unfortunately some provinces do not provide police or crown counsel with guidelines about dealing with this decision in sexual assault cases.

Where the accused is charged and is being dealt with by way of indictment, crown counsel, the judge who conducts the preliminary hearing or the trial judge can later decide that the evidence at the preliminary hearing shows that additional charges should be laid.

The Decision To Lay Charges

Charges are supposed to be laid only in cases where police or crown counsel think that there is a fairly good possibility that the case against the accused can be proven. With government cutbacks, which include cutbacks to the criminal justice system, crown counsel appear to be less willing to take on cases where the odds of getting a conviction are not good. The high costs of trial procedures and the large backlog of cases waiting to be dealt with in the courts are both factors which are considered when deciding whether to proceed with cases.

In provinces where crown counsel lay charges s/he will sometimes ask to see you before deciding whether charges will be laid. This will usually happen only in cases where there is not much evidence other than the information you have given to the police, e.g. there is little or no medical evidence, or no witnesses who saw some of what happened.

You can have a family member or friend go with you to this interview, although crown counsel will usually ask them to wait outside the room. If you would like someone to come into the interview with you, you can ask a rape crisis centre worker to accompany you. She will normally be allowed to be with you in the interview room.

During this interview the crown counsel will be trying to

figure out how you would present the story of what happened in court.

The crown counsel will usually not make the decision about whether to proceed with the charges at the time of the interview with you. Normally s/he will contact you or ask you to contact her or him a short time after the interview.

Once the decision to lay charges has been made, the accused will normally be arrested. If he is being charged with a very minor sexual assault, a summary offence, he may only be sent a summons to appear in court. Once a suspect has been charged he is called 'the accused'.

Unless you have already been in contact with crown counsel the police should contact you to let you know that charges have been laid. However, police sometimes do not bother to contact the victim to let her know what is going on. If some time has gone by and you have not been told about what is going on, you can call up the police officer who interviewed you and ask about what is going on with your case.

What You Can Do If No Charges Are Laid

If the police or crown counsel tell you that they have decided not to proceed with the case, ask the reasons for the decision and write down what reasons are given. If you do not agree with the reasons, you can say why you do not agree. Or you might want to wait and think about what the police or crown counsel said, talk to someone about it, and then phone back and tell them that you do not agree.

Remember that both police and crown counsel are government employees. You have a right to know what is going on with the case and why decisions are being made and they have a duty to tell you. Police and crown counsel are often very busy but it is part of their job to explain things to witnesses. They may use words that you do not understand, or may not explain the procedures very clearly. If you talk with the police or crown counsel and still cannot understand the reasons for the decision you can phone up a rape crisis centre worker and ask her to try and find out what is going on.

If you are not satisfied with the crown counsel's decision you can write a letter to the senior crown counsel for your area, and/or to the Attorney General. The senior crown counsel is called the Regional Crown Counsel or the Senior Crown Attorney in some provinces. The Attorney General is the provincial government minister who is responsible for the criminal justice system.

In your letter say briefly what happened to you and then report what the police or crown counsel decided and the reasons you were given for the decision. Then explain why you do not think the decision was fair. You can also talk about how the decision made you feel. It is important to let people who work in the system know when women do not think that they are being treated fairly. Remember to keep a copy of your letter.

Sometimes the police or crown counsel will decide to lay charges but will lay less serious charges even when the offence was quite serious. When you find out what charges have been laid, look at Appendix I in the back of this book. See if you think the charges that were laid were the ones which fit what happened. If you think that other charges should have been laid, ask why the more serious charges were not laid. If you are not satisfied, tell the police or crown counsel, talk to a rape crisis centre worker and write a letter.

Laying An Information Before A Justice Of The Peace

Section 455 of the Criminal Code provides a way for people, who know or have a good reason to believe that a serious offence has been committed, to start criminal proceedings. If the police or crown counsel have decided not to proceed with the case, and you don't agree with the reasons for that decision, you can go to see the Justice of the Peace.

You can go see the Justice of the Peace who covers the area where the sexual assault took place, or the area where the attacker is living or staying. The Justice of the Peace will have you take the oath and will ask you to put your story in writing.

The Justice of the Peace must then hold a hearing to decide whether there is evidence to back up the information you have given. Witnesses can be asked to come to the hearing. The Justice of the Peace can ask that the man who you are accusing also come to the hearing, but that would be unusual. The attacker does not even have to be told that the hearing is taking place.

In a situation where someone has reported an offence to the police and the investigation was dropped, or where the police or crown counsel decided not to lay charges, the Justice of the Peace will normally talk with the police officers and crown counsel who worked on the case to try to find out the reasons for the decision. If the Justice of the Peace is not satisfied with their reasons s/he may require that the police re-open their investigation. S/he can also ask that a different police officer or crown counsel be assigned to the case. However, it is very uncommon for a Justice of the Peace to overturn a decision on a case by a police officer or crown counsel.

If the Justice of the Peace decides that there is enough evidence to start criminal proceedings s/he can issue a summons to the accused to have him appear to answer the charge. If the Justice of the Peace thinks that the charge is very serious or that the accused might not obey a summons, s/he will issue a warrant to have the accused arrested.

A Justice of the Peace can also give permission to someone who has given information about an offence, to go ahead with a private prosecution. In a private prosecution the victim hires her own lawyer to take the case against her attacker. This way of prosecuting is very unusual and very expensive. Also, if the accused then chooses to be tried by a higher court judge or a judge and jury, the case cannot proceed without the written consent of the Attorney General.

Trying To Get The Charges Dropped

The police or crown counsel have the power to lay charges even if you have decided you do not want to proceed with the case. As employees of the government, police and crown counsel are supposed to act for the good of society. This means that although you may not want to have the charges laid, they may insist on taking steps against the suspect in order to protect society as a whole from someone they think may be dangerous.

If you find out that charges are going to be laid or that they have been laid, and you do not feel that you can go through with all of the legal procedures, you can contact the police or crown counsel directly or you can ask a rape crisis centre worker to help you. Tell the police or crown counsel why you are unable or unwilling to follow through with all the legal procedures. If you have a doctor, a counselor or someone else who is working with you that agrees that you should not have to testify, ask them to contact the police or crown counsel as well.

Usually police and crown counsel will reconsider laying charges, or will consider dropping the charges if the woman is strongly opposed to going ahead with the case. They are aware that it is very difficult to prosecute a case successfully if the woman has to testify against her will. While it is important to remember that if they do decide to go ahead, you can be arrested on a material witness warrant, this would be very unusual in a sexual assault case.

You can also be charged with contempt of court for not coming to the trial, or refusing to answer questions at the trial. If you are charged with contempt of court and are found guilty you can be put in jail. A woman who refused to testify in a rape case in Ontario in 1983 was sentenced to a week in jail. However, people were so angry that a woman who had been raped was being treated that way that judges might be more reluctant to treat other women who refuse to co-operate the same way.

Staying Charges

Crown counsel can, with the consent of the Attorney General, decide to stay the charges at any time after they are laid, but before the accused has been found guilty or not guilty. This is a way of putting the procedure on hold. The crown counsel can decide to restart the proceedings at any time within a year without laying new charges. If more than a year passes and the proceedings are not restarted, the case is treated as though charges were never laid.

Plea Bargaining

Sometimes the accused's lawyer (defence counsel) will talk about the charges with the crown counsel before the hearing. The defence counsel might suggest that the accused would be willing to plead guilty to a less serious charge in exchange for having the more serious charges dropped. The crown counsel will sometimes accept these suggestions. This is called plea bargaining.

Many lawyers do not approve of plea bargaining because it means that decisions do not get made in open court. They suggest that it prevents a case being put to the test in court. Crown counsel will sometimes argue that plea bargaining saves expensive court time and, especially in sexual assault cases, may save a victim who is upset from having to testify in court. Also, the crown counsel may believe that the judge or jury might find the accused not guilty or guilty of only the lesser offence, even after a whole trial.

One of the objections that women have to the use of plea bargaining in sexual assault cases is that the offences that go down on the criminal record of the attacker do not reflect the seriousness of the crime which he committed. For example a man might be charged with sexual assault with a weapon and offer to plead guilty just to sexual assault. If this plea is accepted by the crown only the sexual assault conviction is recorded. This is a way that more violent sexual assaults get forgotten or ignored.

If the accused in your case pleads guilty to a less serious charge and a more serious charge is dropped, you can call up your crown counsel and ask if there was a plea bargain. If s/he says there was no bargain, ask that s/he explain why the more serious charge was dropped. If you are not satisfied with the answer, say so. Talk about the situation with a rape crisis centre worker, and write a letter to the senior crown counsel for your area or to the Attorney General.

Types of Offences

Indictable Offences

Indictable offences are serious offences. An accused who is found guilty of an indictable offence can be sentenced to a wide range of penalties, including years in prison. Because of the seriousness of these offences the procedures are more formal and more complicated than are those for less serious offences. For example, an accused charged with an indictable offence is allowed to choose whether he wants to be tried in a higher court and/or with a jury (see section on *Election By the Accused*).

Most of the procedures described in the rest of this handbook are procedures for indictable offences, except where summary offences are specifically mentioned.

Summary Offences

Summary offences differ from indictable offences in a number of ways, the most important of which is that summary offences carry lower maximum penalties, i.e. they have less serious consequences. Usually the maximum penalties for a summary conviction are six months imprisonment, or a fine of $2,000, or both. Summary offences also have a six-month time limit for starting prosecutions, and are normally dealt with more quickly than indictable offences.

Summary Procedures

A person cannot be arrested without a warrant for a summary offence unless the police officer finds him committing the offence, needs to establish the identity of a person, to preserve evidence or to prevent a repetition of the offence. Where the accused is not arrested he will be sent a summons.

An accused who is charged with a summary offence does not have the right to elect the form of trial. He will be tried in a Provincial Court by a judge alone. He also does not have the right to a preliminary hearing.

Sexual Offences

Most of the offences covering acts of sexual violence are indictable offences. However, there are a few summary offences in the range of what can be called "sexual offences". Doing an indecent act in public or with the intention of offending someone (Section 169), public nudity (Section 170), and indecent or harassing phone calls (subsections 330(2) and 330(3)) are summary offences.

Sexual assault (Section 246.1) is what is called a hybrid offence. A hybrid offence is one which can be dealt with as a summary offence or as an indictable offence. The crown counsel, or in some provinces the police, decide which way an offence under this section will be dealt with. Although this section covers a wide range of behaviour from bottom-pinching to forced sexual intercourse, only the most minor sexual assaults should be dealt with as summary offences.

Young Offenders

Children under the age of twelve years who break the criminal law are not considered responsible for their actions.

Young people who are aged twelve or over but are under eighteen and who commit a criminal offence are usually dealt with under the *Young Offenders Act* (S.C. 1980-81-82, c.110). This act sets out special procedures for young people who are seen as responsible for what they have done, but who are not yet old enough to face the full force of the normal criminal process. These procedures mean that a young offender has most of the same rights as adult offenders but also gets special consideration. For example, the young offender's parents must be told about any proceedings, and they are strongly encouraged to attend. The parents are also allowed to give their opinions to the judge before their child is sentenced.

While many of the procedures in the Youth Courts are the same as those for adults, the Youth Courts are supposed to give more attention to the offender's individual situation and to working out ways of trying to get him to change. This is seen as a better idea than sending young offenders to prison where they will be locked up with older, more experienced offenders. The Youth Courts do not have the power to give out sentences of more than two years in custody for most offences, (three years for very serious offences), or three years for two or more offences.

In cases where a young person has committed a minor offence, the police or other authorities can decide to bypass the formal court process and offer the young person a chance to get involved in a community service program, an education program, counselling sessions, or other activities which they think will be good for the offender and/or the community. In order to get into these programs the young person must admit that he committed the offence and accept responsibility for it.

Where a young person, aged fourteen or older, has committed a very serious offence (which includes most sexual assaults) a youth court judge can decide to transfer him to adult court. A judge will do this if s/he believes that it is necessary in order to protect society, and that the youth should perhaps get a higher sentence than the Youth Court can give.

There are also special provisions in the Criminal Code concerning young persons and sexual offences. Until the law relating to sexual assaults was changed in 1983, males under the age of fourteen were seen as not being able to commit rape. Even now someone under the age of fourteen cannot be tried for the offences of sexual exploitation (Section 140), invitation to sexual touching (Section 141), or exposing his genitals to a person under the age of fourteen (Section 169(2)).

In addition, where someone under the age of sixteen is charged with committing any of these offences, or with sexual assault (Section 246.1) against someone who is between twelve and fourteen years old, but not more than two years younger than the assailant, and who is not under his authority or dependent on him, the accused can raise the defence of consent. This means that in this situation the accused cannot be convicted unless it is proven beyond a reasonable doubt that the victim did not consent. These provisions were included in the recent legal changes to try to make sure that young people who both choose be involved in sexual activity would not be subject to criminal penalties. However, they also have the effect of placing a greater burden on a young victim who happens to have been sexually assaulted by someone only slightly older.

The Arrest

In order to be able to arrest someone the police must first believe that a crime has taken place or is about to take place. They must also have 'reasonable and probable' grounds to believe that he has committed or is about to commit an offence.

If you are able to give the police enough information for them to be able to identify the attacker, they may try to pick him up for questioning right away. Often they will try to gather all the evidence and talk to other witnesses before they go out to question the person who is suspected.

In a situation where you do not know the name of the attacker the police will work to try to identify him through checking car licence plate numbers, fingerprints, checking descriptions they have on file, etc.

Sometimes police will contact people they suspect and ask them to come in for questioning. In this situation the person does not have to agree to be questioned, although if he refuses the police may wonder why he is not co-operating.

The police can only arrest the suspect if they decide they have grounds to believe that the person has committed the offence. If they do arrest someone without these grounds they can be sued for wrongful arrest.

When the police arrest someone they have to tell him why he is being arrested and they must tell him of his right to contact a lawyer. The police can ask him about the offence they believe that he committed but he does not have to answer any of their questions.

If charges have not already been laid, they normally must be laid within 24 hours of the arrest. If the accused is being charged with a less serious offence the police can decide to release him. They will not release him if they think he should be detained in order to protect the public, to preserve evidence, to establish his identity or to make sure that he appears for court. If he is released, there may well be a no-contact order or other conditions attached to his release.

In cases involving sexual assaults, where the police or crown counsel have decided to deal with the assault as a summary offence, the accused might not be arrested. Instead he might be sent a notice saying that he must appear in court at a later date.

Bail

In cases of minor sexual assaults (See Appendix I subsection 246.1(b)) the police can decide to release someone who they have arrested and charged. For all other sexual assaults the person who has been arrested and charged will be detained. However, an accused cannot be held more than 24 hours unless he is brought before a judge. If a judge is not available within 24 hours he must be brought before a judge as soon as possible. The hearing to decide whether he will be held in custody or released can be delayed for up to three days. Any further delay must be with the permission of the accused.

Because people in Canada have the legal right to be presumed innocent until they are proven guilty, those accused of crimes are not usually held in jail until the trial. To decide whether someone should be held or released a 'bail' hearing takes place. 'Bail' is the old word for what is now called 'judicial interim release'.

The Bail Hearing

You and any members of the public are allowed to attend the bail hearing. However it usually takes place soon after the arrest and does not last very long.

At this hearing the Crown Counsel may try to 'show cause', which means to give reasons as to why the accused should be held in custody. There are two reasons which can be used to keep an accused in custody. The first is where the Crown Counsel can show that there is a good chance that the accused will not come to the preliminary hearing or trial. The second reason is where the Crown Counsel can convince the judge that letting the accused go would be against the public interest or would endanger the public safety. To use this second reason the Crown Counsel has to show that the accused might commit another criminal offence while he is out waiting for the trial.

The Crown Counsel or the accused's lawyer can submit

evidence or call witnesses at the bail hearing. The judge can consider the background, living situation, employment status, and any criminal record of the accused when deciding whether or not he should be kept in custody. The accused can be asked to testify at a bail hearing but he cannot be asked questions about the offence he is accused of having committed.

In cases where the accused is already out on bail for another serious offence, or is not a resident of Canada, or is already charged with failing to appear for another hearing or trial, or is charged with breaking a bail condition, it is the accused or his lawyer who have to 'show cause', to give good reasons why he should be let out.

If the accused or his lawyer asks the judge to refuse to allow the press to report what goes on at the bail hearing, the judge must grant this request. The press may still report the name of the accused, the offences with which he is charged and the result of the hearing, as well as certain other basic information such as the names of the judge, Crown Counsel, and defense counsel.

Release With Conditions

A judge can also decide that an accused should be released, but that the release should be on certain conditions. Where the accused does not normally live in Canada, the judge must place conditions on his release. Some examples of conditions that the judge can use are that the accused must not communicate with any witnesses in the case, or that he has to report to the police station at certain times, or that he can't leave the city or town.

If the judge believes that it is necessary, the accused can be required to post a bond to back up his promise that he will appear for the trial. A bond is a promise to pay a certain amount of money if the accused does not show up for the trial, or breaks a condition of his bail. The judge can only make the accused put up cash or property if the accused lives more than 200 kilometres from the court.

The judge can also require the accused to find someone else to act as a surety. A surety is someone who will post a bond for the accused as a way of saying that they will take responsibility for the accused's behaviour while he is out waiting for the trial.

No-Contact Provision

Most women who have been sexually assaulted think that if the accused is released it should be on the condition that he have no contact with them. This is called a *'no-contact provision'*. If the accused has a no-contact provision as a condition of his release and he makes contact with you anyway, he can be charged with breaking his bail conditions and can be arrested again. No-contact provisions can also cover your friends or family. In some places no-contact provisions are obtained automatically in cases of sexual assault, in other places they must be asked for. If you would feel more safe if the accused in your case had a no-contact provision as a condition of his release, ask the police or the Crown Counsel who are dealing with your case to make this request to the judge.

Either the accused's lawyer or the Crown Counsel can ask a higher court judge to review the decision of a judge in a bail hearing.

Changing Bail Conditions

Normally the conditions decided upon by a judge at a bail hearing will apply until the trial is over or, where the accused is found guilty, until he has been sentenced. The judge who decided the conditions of release usually cannot decide to change those conditions. However a judge who is hearing the case as a preliminary hearing or trial can, if reasons are given which show that it is necessary, change the bail conditions.

Where an accused has been held in custody for 90 days (30 days in the case of a summary offence) and the trial has not yet begun, the person in charge of the prison where he is being held must apply for another hearing to decide whether the accused should be released. If the judge decides that the delay is unfair and that it is not necessary to keep the accused in custody, s/he can order that the accused be released. S/he can also order that the accused continue to be held, if necessary, and give directions to have the trial held as soon as possible.

Breaking Conditions of Bail

If the judge believes that an accused has broken the condition of his release, s/he can issue a warrant for his arrest. A police officer can arrest someone who has broken the conditions of his bail without a warrant. An accused who has been arrested for breach of his bail conditions will have another hearing. If, at the hearing, the judge is convinced that the accused broke or was about to break the conditions of release, or that he committed another serious criminal offence while out on bail, the judge must order that he be detained in custody, unless the accused can show a good reason why he should be released again.

Getting Information About Your Case

Often people who work in the criminal justice system do not understand that someone who has been sexually assaulted might want to be kept informed about what is going on with her case. This is partly because they do not see it as your case. They see you as one of a number of witnesses.

If you want to know about what is going on in the case you can contact the police officers who interviewed you. If you were interviewed by detectives, contact the detectives. If you have been told the name of the crown counsel who is dealing with the case, you can call the crown counsel.

If you can't get hold of anyone actually working on the case you can call up the Court Clerk's office in the area where the offence took place. In order for them to check the files you will have to give them the name of the accused and the date that the offence took place. When they find the file they should be able to tell you the offences with which he was charged, whether he is out on bail, and the conditions of bail, if any. The clerk may also be able to tell you the date of any hearings which have been set, and the room in which the hearing will take place. Remember to ask for the case file number as well.

If you have the date of the hearing and the court room number, you can call up the crown counsel office and find out the name of the crown counsel who will be working on the case.

Waiting for the Next Step

One of the most difficult things about going through a sexual assault trial is the long periods of waiting for the next part of the procedure. The time between the accused being charged and the beginning of the preliminary hearing can be six months or even more. The trial will sometimes not take place until a year after the preliminary hearing. In smaller communities delays tend not to be as long, but in the cities and large towns the courts have a large backlog of cases which causes the long wait.

Sometimes dates will be set for hearings and then there will be another delay. This can be very frustrating. Many women try to get themselves emotionally prepared to testify and then feel let down when it is put off. Lots of women just want to get the procedures over with so that they can get on with their lives. Although it is very difficult, try to avoid putting your life on hold for the months of waiting. The time will pass more quickly if you try to carry on with your life.

Remembering Details

Many women are worried that they will forget some of the details about what happened during the months that they are waiting for the preliminary hearing. Writing down as much as you can remember about what happened can help you keep track of the details. Having the information written down might also help you to feel like you don't have to think about it all the time.

Nobody's memory is perfect. There are things that you will forget or not be sure of. That is normal, and people will understand. As time passes you may suddenly remember some detail; the colour of something the attacker was wearing, something he said to you, or something about the place where the sexual assault took place. Write these things down and tell the crown counsel about them during your interview. Often crown counsel will give you a copy of the statement you made to the police to read over before the hearing to help refresh your memory.

Change Of Address

If you move or go away for a long period of time, it is a good idea to tell the police and/or crown counsel. Sometimes a hearing will be set with only a few weeks notice, so the crown counsel will need to know where you are in order to send you a subpoena.

If You Change Your Mind

Some women report the sexual assault to the police, and even go through the preliminary hearing, but at some point find that they just can't go through with the trial. While you do not have a legal right to drop the case, you can talk to the crown counsel about dropping the charges if you feel unable or unwilling to go through with the rest of the procedures. (See *Trying To Get The Charges Dropped*.)

Interview with Crown Counsel

Usually three to six months after charges have been laid you will be asked to attend an interview with crown counsel.

The Role Of Crown Counsel

The crown counsel is a lawyer who is employed by government to deal with cases where people are charged with a criminal offence. The crown counsel is also called the prosecutor or the crown attorney. The crown counsel is the formal representative of the Queen (the Crown) and s/he is supposed to act on behalf of society as a whole. It is not the job of the crown to prove that the accused is guilty, but to try and find out the truth about what happened and to present it to the court.

The crown counsel is not your lawyer. Although it may seem strange, the victim of an offence is, in official terms, a witness to what happened. To the crown counsel and to the courts you are a witness. You may wonder why the man who attacked you gets to have a lawyer to defend him in court while you do not have anyone to defend you. Many women think that this is unfair.

As far as the criminal justice system is concerned you are in the courtroom as someone who has information to give about a crime that was committed. You are not charged with a crime. As a witness you will be called on to testify, to tell your story to the court. Often women who are sexually assaulted are shocked to find out that they are seen as just a witness in the case.

The defense counsel will probably challenge what you say and will ask you lots of very difficult questions. Many women feel like it is they who are being prosecuted. You may feel like you wish someone was there to defend you. It is the job of the crown counsel and of the judge to make sure that you are not asked questions which are not relevant or which are abusive.

Having Your Own Representative

Any witness can hire her own lawyer to be present in the

courtroom. This is sometimes done in cases where the witness is concerned that there might be some evidence which shows that she may also have committed some crime. If you are a witness your lawyer will probably not be granted status in the courtroom. It is therefore expensive and usually not very useful to have your lawyer be present.

If you think that you would like someone who understands the legal procedures with you at court, you can contact a rape crisis centre. Rape crisis centres sometimes have women who are available during the day to go with women to court. This way you will have someone to answer your questions as you think of them.

You can also ask the crown counsel about things that you don't understand. It is better for the crown's case to have witnesses who are not feeling lost or confused, so feel free to ask your crown counsel about the procedures.

The defence counsel might also interview the crown witnesses before the trial, although this does not often happen. If the defence counsel wants to interview you, you should talk to the crown counsel about it first. You are not under any obligation to be interviewed by the defence counsel if you don't want to.

Before The Interview With Crown Counsel

The crown counsel first comes into contact with a case through the police file. S/he looks over the information in the file and, in some provinces, decides whether there is enough evidence to lay a charge. As mentioned before, the crown will sometimes want to interview some of the witnesses before making this decision.

In many cases you will have two crown counsel, one for a preliminary hearing, and another for the trial in a higher court. This is because there are two groups of crown counsel in two offices; those who usually work in the provincial courts and those who usually work in the higher courts. If you feel strongly that you would like the same crown counsel for both the preliminary hearing and the trial you can tell the crown counsel, but the offices do not often make these arrangements.

Usually you will not meet with the crown until a week or two before the preliminary hearing or trial. You will be sent a subpoena which is a notice asking you to appear at a court at a certain time to give your evidence. You will also be phoned or sent a notice asking you to meet with crown counsel sometime before you go to court. If you still have not heard from crown counsel a week or so before the hearing, you can call up the crown counsel and ask to arrange a time for your interview. (To find out the name of the crown counsel who is working on your case see the section on *Getting Information About Your Case*).

While you are waiting for this interview you can write down any questions you might want to ask. You can also arrange for a friend, family member or rape crisis centre worker to go with you, although the crown counsel will not usually let anyone else but a rape crisis centre worker be with you during the interview.

The Interview

The interview with crown counsel has two main purposes; to prepare you to testify and to enable the crown counsel to prepare his or her case. In the discussion with you the crown counsel will probably ask you to tell your story again. You will be asked to try to be very clear and very specific. You will be asked to tell what you remember as best you can. Nobody expects you to remember everything. If there are things that you don't remember you can say so.

The crown counsel might also ask you to accompany him/her to the place where the sexual assault took place, although this is very rare. This may be done so that s/he can get a better idea of what happened.

The interview will also help the crown counsel to get an idea of what you will say in court and how you will say it. Sometimes crown counsel will ask you the sort of questions you will be asked by the defence. Some crown counsel do this because they say that it gives the witness an idea of the sorts of difficult questions they will be asked in the court. If the questions are upsetting you, you can say so.

Sometimes people who work in the criminal justice system forget or ignore the personal nature of the attack, and the strong feelings that the victim has about the procedures that follow. It is all right to remind a crown counsel that you have strong feelings about what happened and about what is going to happen.

It is fair to ask the crown to take those feelings into consideration. It is also fair to ask that the crown counsel explain the procedures clearly.

Special Procedures

If you have had any problems with the accused, if he has made contact with you, or has threatened or harassed you, be sure to tell the crown counsel at this time.

You should also use the interview to talk about the special procedures related to sexual assault cases. If you want the trial to take place in another town (this is called changing the venue) or if you want the public to be kept out of the courtroom, use this interview to tell the crown counsel your reasons. S/he can only make an application to the judge for a change of venue or excluding the public from the courtroom. It is the judge who has the final decision.

If you want to affirm (which means to promise to tell the truth but not swear on the bible) when you are called as a witness, tell this to the crown counsel. If you do not want to state your address out loud in court, also let the crown counsel know.

Some crown counsel will give women a copy of their statement to the police or of the transcripts (written records) of the preliminary hearing to read. You can read these over before the hearing or trial to refresh your memory, but you should not try to memorize them. You are being asked to tell your story on the witness stand, not to recite a written record of it. If you are given copies of your statement or a transcript, avoid showing them to, or talking about them with, anyone else.

It is important to remember that the crown counsel does not see himself or herself as *your* lawyer, but as representing the interests of society as a whole. But this does not mean that the crown counsel should not treat you with respect. If you find that you are unable to communicate your concerns or that your questions are not being answered, try calling a rape crisis centre worker for back-up. If need be you can write a letter to the senior crown counsel for the area or to the Attorney General.

Election by the Accused

In most cases the person who is charged with a serious (indictable) offence has the right to decide the kind of trial he will have. This is called electing the form of trial.

In a case where the prosecutor has decided to proceed summarily the accused has no right to choose which way he will be tried. He will be tried in a provincial court by a judge without a jury.

The Attorney General can require that an accused be tried by a judge and jury if he is charged with an offence which carries a maximum sentence of more than five years imprisonment.

If an accused does not show up on the date set for his trial, and he cannot give the judge a good reason for not showing up, he will lose his right to a jury trial and will be tried by a judge alone.

To elect the form of trial the accused will be brought in front of a judge and asked whether he wants to be tried by a provincial court judge, or by a higher court judge, or by a higher court judge and a jury.

Where an accused chooses to be tried by a provincial court judge, the judge will ask the accused to plead guilty or not guilty to the charge. Unless the accused pleads guilty the judge will either hold the trial or set a later date for the trial.

If he chooses to be tried by a higher court judge or a higher court judge and a jury, the judge will either hold a preliminary hearing right away or will set a date for a hearing.

More Than One Accused

If there are two or more accused who have been charged in relation to the same offence they will each be asked how they want to be tried. If they do choose different modes of trial a judge can overrule their decisions and require that they be tried by a higher court judge and jury.

Normally people who are charged jointly with the same offence are tried together, but a judge can allow people who are charged with the same offence to have separate trials if s/he finds that it is in the interests of justice. Sometimes a person who is charged jointly with another person will want a separate trial in case there is some evidence which can be used only against the other person. A separate trial would ensure that the judge and/or jury in his trial would not even hear this evidence.

Changing An Election

An accused person can change his election. He can decide to be tried in a higher court and then, during or after the preliminary hearing, change to a provincial court. This is a way that the accused and his lawyer can get to hear the prosecution evidence before the trial but still have the trial in a lower court. Hearing the prosecution evidence helps them prepare the defence case.

Surviving Procedures After A Sexual Assault

Courtroom Personnel

The Judge

The judge is appointed by the government. Provincial court judges are appointed by the provincial government. Higher court judges are chosen by the federal government. The judge is someone who has legal training and has worked as a lawyer. Judges generally do not specialize in particular types of cases and are therefore unlikely to have special knowledge, other than legal knowledge, about sexual assault.

It is the task of the judge to decide questions of law. S/he will decide which information can be used as evidence in the case. S/he also decides whether the questions you are asked are appropriate and must be answered. Where a jury is present the judge will decide what evidence the jury can hear and will, at the end of the trial, instruct the jury about the legal points which apply to the case.

If there is no jury the judge will also decide the facts of the case, which means that s/he will decide whether the accused is innocent or guilty. The judge will also decide the sentence of the accused if he is convicted.

The judge sits on an elevated platform at the front of the courtroom, often with a coat of arms or the Queen's picture on the wall behind. In a provincial court or County Court the judge will be called "Your Honour". In the higher courts the judges are called "My Lord" or "My Lady" and are referred to as "Mr. or Madam Justice . . .". Usually the judge will be wearing robes, although this is not required in a provincial court.

The Crown Counsel

The crown counsel is the lawyer who presents the case against the accused. Except in the provincial court, the crown counsel wears robes. The crown counsel will sometimes have an assistant.

The Defence Counsel

The defence counsel is a lawyer hired by the accused to

present evidence and argue the case on his behalf. The defence counsel is paid by the accused or, where he cannot afford a lawyer, by Legal Aid. The defence counsel will wear robes in all but the Provincial Court and will also sometimes have an assistant.

The Court Clerk

The Court Clerk will also wear robes in the higher courts. It is the job of the court clerk to call the court to order, to read the charges against the accused, and to swear in the witnesses. The Court Clerk has the responsibility for taking care of the exhibits and official court documents.

The Court Stenographer

The Court Stenographer, also known as the Court recorder, takes down everything that is said during the proceedings. S/he will either record by hand or will use tape recording or stenographic equipment.

The Sheriffs

The Sheriffs are always in uniform. They are in the courtroom to provide security and to maintain order. If the accused is being held in custody they will escort him to and from the courtroom.

The Jury

Where the accused decides (elects) to be tried by judge and jury, there will be twelve people sitting in two rows along the side of the courtroom to the judge's left. The jury is supposed to represent a reasonable group of people in society. Their task is to weigh the evidence which is put before them and to decide the facts of the case. This means that they must decide which they think is the true version of what happened. All of them must come to an agreement on whether the guilt of the accused has been proven beyond a reasonable doubt.

Before the trial a panel of people are called to appear for jury duty. The sheriff then writes the name of each panel member on a card and puts it in a box. In the court the court clerk will shake the box and pull out cards one at a time and call out the name on each card until s/he believes that there are enough to form a jury, after allowing for challenges. The court clerk swears in each member of the jury in the order in which their names were called.

Both the crown counsel and the accused can challenge jurors. Challenging jurors means that they can have them removed from the jury. The crown counsel and defence can each remove a number of jurors without cause, which means without giving any reason.

A judge can discharge a juror (remove him or her from the jury) because of illness or for another good reason. A juror can also be discharged, for example, if s/he is seen talking with the accused or other witnesses. If a juror is discharged the trial can continue as long as the number of jurors does not drop below ten.

The jurors may be kept together until they decide the verdict, or the judge may allow them to separate during the times when the trial is adjourned. It is a criminal offence for a juror to give out any information about the discussions of the jurors when they were out of the courtroom. It is also contempt of court to talk with a jury member about a case being tried.

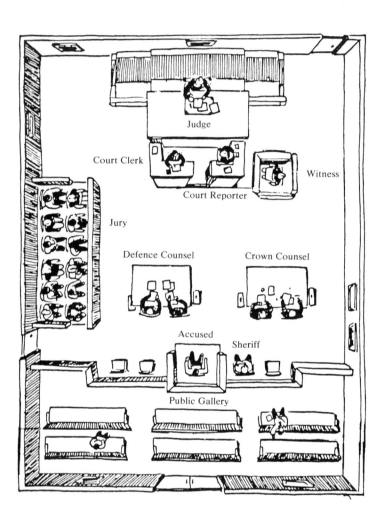

This is a basic diagram of a courtroom used for criminal trials.

Surviving Procedures After A Sexual Assault

Information on Being a Witness

You are the main witness for the Crown in the preliminary hearing or trial. In the courtroom you will usually be referred to as 'the witness'.

A witness must almost always appear to give her evidence in person. Even if the evidence of a young victim has been video-taped, and the videotape is to be used in court, she will have to testify. Only where a victim or a witness is under the age of eighteen will the judge sometimes allow her to testify outside the courtroom, so she does not have to give her evidence in front of her attacker. But this will be permitted only where the judge believes that it would be necessary in order to get the young person to tell the whole story of what happened, and only where the court has the facilities so that the judge and/or jury can watch the testimony on closed-circuit television or by some other method.

Evidence from a witness who has given evidence at a prelim-inary hearing, but who cannot or will not appear at the trial to give evidence, can sometimes be read into the record of a trial. However, this evidence will almost always be challenged by the defence counsel and will only rarely be accepted by the court.

As a witness you will be outside the courtroom while the other witnesses are giving their testimony. This is so that what you say about what happened will not be influenced by what others have said about it. For this reason it is important that you do not discuss your testimony or other peoples' testimony with anyone else until the trial is over.

If you do discuss the testimony, or even if it appears that you have discussed the testimony, the judge can stop the proceedings, decide there has been a mistrial (a serious problem in the hearing or trial), and require that there be a new trial which will start again from the beginning. Having to start again is both time-consuming and expensive. It will mean that you will have to give your testimony again. It is much better to be very careful to not talk about your testimony or the testimony of other witnesses until the proceedings are over, than to risk a mistrial.

Being Called As A Witness

You will be sent a summons which will tell you the date, time and place of the preliminary hearing. If you are being asked to give evidence at a trial, a sheriff or a police officer will bring you a document called a subpoena which requires you to appear for the trial. If you are sent a summons or subpoena your employer must allow you the time off work you need to go to court. You do not, however, get paid for the time off work unless it is covered in your union contract or your employer agrees.

If you are sent a summons or subpoena and do not show up to give evidence the judge can issue a warrant for your arrest. If you have decided that you cannot or do not want to testify, contact your crown counsel, if possible before you are sent a summons or subpoena.

Before You Are Called To Testify

In the day or so before the hearing it is a good idea to think over what happened. If the crown counsel has given you a copy of your statement, or if you have made your own notes, read them over. Make sure that you remember the date, time and place of the attack. Try and go through the events and make sure that you are clear about the order in which they happened. Try and remember what was said to whom, colours, lighting, times, distances, etc.

Sometimes you will also be asked to meet with the crown counsel a second time just before the hearing or trial. If not, just go to the courtroom where the trial is being held. If you arrive late go and find a sheriff who will go and tell the crown counsel that you have arrived.

You do not need to go into the courtroom. At the opening of the trial there will be an "Order for the exclusion of witnesses". This means that all the witnesses must leave the courtroom. This is done to make sure that the witnesses are not influenced by the testimony of other witnesses before giving their own. If you have gone in to the courtroom you must leave after this order has been made.

Your friends or family can either go in the courtroom or wait with you, but they should not go back and forth from the courtroom to where you are waiting. If they do go in the courtroom you must not discuss with them anything which has been said in the courtroom.

You should wait in the general area of the courtroom where the hearing or trial is being held. If the accused is not in custody he might be waiting in the same area. If you do not want to see him ask your crown counsel or a sheriff if you can wait in a witness room. Only some courthouses have witness rooms. If there is no witness room available, ask where there is another place you can wait.

Your Testimony

When you are called to testify, go into the courtroom and go to the witness box. While you are still standing the court clerk will swear you in. After you have been sworn in the judge will ask you to sit down. If you do not want to take the oath and say 'so help me God', you can choose to affirm. Affirming means that you promise to tell the truth but that you don't refer to a god. If you have decided that you want to affirm it is helpful to tell the crown counsel beforehand. You may also choose to swear on a holy book other than the bible.

You will be asked to say your name and may be asked to state your address. If you don't want to give your address in front of the accused, you can ask to write it down and give it to the court clerk. If you want to give your address this way, try to remember to tell the crown counsel during your interview before the hearing or trial.

You will then be questioned by the crown counsel. This is called examination in chief. You are simply expected to tell your story in your own words, being as clear about the details of what happened as you can be. The crown counsel already knows your story and will ask you questions about what happened, usually in the order in which it happened.

Direct your answers to the judge. If you have to speak to the judge, you can call him/her "Your Honour" (if it is a Provincial Court) or "My Lord" or "My Lady" (if it is a higher court).

Speak more loudly than you would normally. The microphone in front of you is not to amplify your voice but is used for tape recording the proceedings. Try to speak more slowly and more clearly than usual as the judge will be making notes of what you say. Do not assume that the judge and jury know anything about your case; they are hearing it for the first time.

When you are asked a question try to just answer the question and to avoid giving information which is not part of the answer to that question. Be as clear and as specific as you can be, but remember that no one remembers every detail. If you don't understand a question you can ask that it be repeated. You can take as much time as you need to answer each question.

Avoid using phrases like "I think" or "I guess". If you are sure that something happened, say so. If you are not sure, say "I'm not sure" or "I don't remember". If you are sure that you didn't see something, say "I did not see. . .". If you are asked for your opinion on something and you don't feel that you want to give one, you can say, "I can't give an opinion on that".

You will probably find it very difficult to talk about what happened to you when the man who did it is right there. It is sometimes easier if you look at the judge (who is sitting in the opposite direction from the accused) when you are giving your testimony, or you can look at the jury. You may also want to look over at your friends, family or rape crisis centre worker if they are sitting in the courtroom. However, sometimes if you continue to look at them through the cross-examination the defence counsel will stand in the way so that you can't see each other.

Identifying The Attacker

Usually you will be asked to identify the attacker. Often you will just be asked whether he is in the courtroom, and, if he is, to point to him. This is the only time that you must look at him. If the identity of the attacker is an issue in the trial, that is, if the accused is saying that it was not him but someone else who attacked you, you will be asked to describe everything you remember about the attacker at the time of the attack. You will then be asked whether he is in the courtroom. If you state that he is in the courtroom you will be asked where he is seated, and to point to him and to describe what he is wearing.

Cross-Examination

When the crown counsel has finished questioning you, the defence counsel will ask you more questions. This is called cross-examination. Where there is more than one accused, and they are being tried together they may each have a lawyer who will ask you questions.

The defence counsel will often ask questions about details which may seem unreasonably picky. Try to answer them as best you can. Sometimes the defence counsel will ask these sorts of questions to try and suggest that your memory is not very good. This is a common tactic. Just try to stay calm and when you do not know the answer or are not sure, say so.

If you are not sure about whether you have to answer a question you can ask the judge whether it is necessary.

If you refuse to answer questions which the judge at the preliminary hearing has decided that you can be asked, the judge has the power to imprison you for up to eight days. If, after eight days, you still refuse to answer s/he can imprison you for additional periods of eight days until you agree to answer. While it is probably unlikely that a sexual assault victim would be sent to prison for refusing to answer questions, it is important to remember that judges do have this power.

Self-Incrimination

Section 13 of the Charter of Rights and Freedoms (Constitution Act, 1982) gives protection against self-incrimination to all witnesses. This means that you have the right not to have any incriminating evidence (evidence which makes it appear that you are guilty of committing an offence) used against you in any other proceedings.

If you are asked a question, and you believe that the answer would incriminate you, you can object to the question. The judge can then order you to answer the question, but your answer cannot be used against you in other proceedings, for example in a criminal trial charging you with an offence.

This protection does not apply to people who are charged with perjury or giving contradictory statements.

Perjury

Perjury is where a witness in a judicial proceeding gives false evidence (information that is not true and which s/he knows is not true) with the intention of being misleading. Perjury is regarded as a serious crime and carries a maximum penalty of fourteen years imprisonment.

Witnesses who are not taking part in a judicial proceeding but who are making a sworn statement and who make a statement which they know is false can be charged with making a false statement (Section 122 of the Criminal Code). This charge also carries a maximum penalty of fourteen years.

A witness who makes contradictory statements in a judicial proceeding can be charged under Section 124 of the Criminal Code. An example of this would be where someone said one thing at a preliminary hearing and a very different thing at the trial which followed. Again, a person can only be convicted under this section if s/he intended to be misleading. The maximum penalty for this offence is also fourteen years imprisonment.

Generally people find that being on a witness stand is very stressful. It is very important to think very carefully about what you say. Take your time and be clear. The above sections of the Criminal Code will not be used against anyone who gets confused. They will only be used where it can be proven that the witness lied intentionally.

After Testifying

When you have finished your testimony the judge will excuse you. If you have been testifying at a preliminary hearing you must leave the courtroom. If you have been testifying at a trial it is usually all right to stay in the courtroom to watch the trial after you have been excused. However, sometimes crown counsel or defence counsel will need to recall a witness. If there is a possibility that you will be recalled you cannot stay in the courtroom. Check with your crown counsel to see whether it is possible that you will be recalled.

Witness Fees

Some provinces provide small witness fees to people testifying in court for criminal matters. Other provinces provide expenses for meals, transportation, childcare and, where necessary, accommodation. Accommodation allowance may have to be approved beforehand. You will probably have to provide receipts in order to claim for transportation and/or childcare.

As different courts have different ways of dealing with witness expense money, ask crown counsel or a sheriff how to claim your expenses.

You cannot claim for time you have lost from work (but see section on *Criminal Injury Compensation*).

Media Coverage

Canada follows a tradition of keeping the courts open to the public, and in modern times, to the public through the media. Parliament has made some exceptions to this rule in order to protect the accused from media reports which might prejudice people against him before he is proven guilty.

Because victims of sexual assault face a strong prejudice, and often have a great fear of disclosing the violence against them, they also have been given some protection from the media.

Generally the media will not print or broadcast the name of a victim of sexual assault. After a sexual assault has happened they may hear about it by someone calling in, or through a police announcement. The police can say that a sexual assault happened at a certain place. If the attacker has been charged they may give out his name. They may give the age and/or occupation of the victim, but they should not disclose her name or any information which would identify her.

Request By The Accused For A Ban On Publication

If the accused or his lawyer requests that the media not be allowed to cover the proceedings of a bail hearing or of a preliminary hearing the judge must grant the request. This means that the media cannot publish or broadcast information about the accusations made, the evidence which was given, or the reasons that the accused was detained or released. Where the judge grants this kind of request the order stays in effect until either the accused is discharged after a preliminary hearing or the trial is over.

Where the accused has given a confession or has admitted some part of the offence, and this is brought out at a preliminary hearing, the media cannot publish or broadcast the fact that the confession or admission was made until the accused has been discharged at the end of the preliminary hearing or the trial is over. This rule applies even when the accused or his lawyer have not requested a ban on publication.

The media are allowed to print or broadcast the name of the accused, the offences with which he has been charged, the names of the lawyers and the judge, the result of the hearing, and any information which they may have received from other sources.

Request By The Victim For A Ban On Publication

Subsection 442(3.1) of the Criminal Code sets out a special protection for victims of sexual offences and for witnesses under the age of eighteen in proceedings regarding sexual offences. According to this subsection the judge must, at the beginning of the preliminary hearing or trial, tell the victim or witness under eighteen that they have the right to apply for an order which will prohibit the media from publishing or broadcasting their name or any other information which might disclose their identity.

If it looks like the judge is not going to bring up the question of a ban on publication, you or the crown counsel can make the request. If you make this request and the media publishes it anyway they are committing an offence.

Talking To The Media

Sometimes women who are going through, or have gone through a sexual assault trial will feel like they want people to know what it is really like. Talking to the media is a way to get this information out to the largest number of people.

The media has a mixed history of reporting sexual assault cases. Most sexual assault cases are not even covered in the media. Many reports focus only on the most sensational aspects of the case. This can leave a sexual assault victim feeling as though something which is very personal to her has been spread all over the press. Or she may feel that what happened has been twisted by reporters. Only sometimes will reporters cover a trial in a way which is respectful of the victim.

No witnesses should speak to members of the media while the trial is going on, i.e. before the verdict has come down (which means that the accused has been found either guilty or not guilty). A victim impact statement (see section on *Sentencing*) is one way of having your point of view heard in the courtroom, and one way of reporters getting to hear your feelings about what has happened.

If you think that the coverage of your trial has been really biased you can wait until the trial is over and then call up the reporter and say so. Explain to the reporter why the coverage was unfair, using specific examples from the stories s/he produced. If the reporter does not seem to understand what you are saying, or is rude, you can phone or write to the editor (in the case of a newspaper) or producer (in the case of radio or television). If you do not feel able to call the reporter, you can ask a rape crisis centre worker to call for you.

After the verdict you are free to talk with reporters. Sometimes, however, the media will not publish or broadcast comments from witnesses until after the accused has been sentenced, or even until after an appeal has been heard. The practice varies from case to case.

If you do decide to talk to the media remember that they can print or broadcast almost anything that you say to them. Remember also that they may use what you say in a way which is different than you intended. Some reporters are better than others, and some are more respectful of women than are others. You might want to contact a rape crisis centre to see if they know anyone in the media who is particularly good to talk to.

Special Rules of Evidence for Sexual Offences

The special rules for sexual offences which developed over hundreds of years show a strong bias against women. These rules were really rules which singled out women who had been victims of sexual violence. The rules implied that these women are less trustworthy than other witnesses.

That these rules continued for so long shows the influence of the myths about rape. These myths are that women falsely 'cry rape', that women like being raped, that 'nice girls' don't get raped, or that women 'ask for it'. Rape was seen primarily as an act of sexual intercourse and not as an act of violence.

During the last ten years or more, women have challenged these myths. Stories told to rape crisis centre workers, and the findings of many studies, showed that these myths are not true. People started to understand that sexual assault is a terrible, violent crime and that no woman wants to be raped. As a result, some of the rules which were so clearly unfair to victims of sexual assault have been changed. Some have not yet been changed.

The Issue Of Consent

The special rules which still remain are rules which relate to the question of whether the woman consented to the man's actions. Because most rapes involve a situation where there are no other witnesses to what took place, and because heterosexual intercourse is seen as a normal activity, the usual response of a man who is charged with rape is to say that sex did take place but that the woman agreed to it. The question of consent then becomes the major issue in the trial.

The issue of consent is complicated. Men in our society are brought up to be aggressive. Being aggressive is usually seen as 'being a man'. This aggression carries over into the way men relate to women. Men are taught that they must 'make the first move', and that if the woman says no she really means yes.

Pornography teaches men that women are available for sex; that women really want to be persuaded to have sex; and that being 'forceful' is part of playing the game. Some men do not even believe that a woman has the right to say no. Some men think that they have the right to overpower women, that that is part of 'being a man'.

Many men believe that there are 'good' women and 'bad' women. A 'bad' woman can be anyone who acts independently or somehow does not fit the man's image of the proper female role. Some of these men believe that 'bad' women are fair game, that they can do whatever they want to these women.

It is because of these different beliefs about sexuality that the issue of consent in a sexual assault trial is so difficult.

Many women who have been raped think it is bizarre that the men who raped them later say that they consented. To these women the idea that other people, i.e. the judge and jury, might believe that they consented is both humiliating and puzzling. In a court of law, however, the prosecution must prove 'beyond a reasonable doubt' that the woman did not consent. If the judge or members of the jury continue to have doubts, they have to find the accused not guilty.

The special rules are tools which the defence can use to raise these doubts in the minds of the judge and jury. These rules and the myths about women and sexual violence continue to play an important role in trials of sexual offences.

The changes to the Criminal Code which came into effect in 1983 included a new subsection on consent. This subsection says that where the victim gives in to the attacker because she or someone else is threatened or forced, or because the attacker is fraudulent (which means that he lies to her about what he's doing), or he uses his authority against her, for example, as her employer, this is not real consent.

This new subsection is important because it recognizes that women are sometimes pressured by men who have power over them. It also acknowledges that many women are too frightened to fight back, or they fear they will be seriously hurt unless they give in, and that this is not the same as consent.

However the changes in 1983 also brought the inclusion of the defence of honest belief in the Criminal Code. This reflected past decisions of the courts which held that if a man honestly believed a woman was consenting to have sex he could not be convicted, even if she really was not consenting. This belief does not have to be reasonable. The problem is, of course, that many men really do believe that women want to be coerced into having sex. However, an accused cannot simply just say that he had an honest belief in consent, he must show that there is some evidence of his belief before the defence will be put to the jury. Nevertheless, this provision means that women who have actually had sexual actions forced upon them may be found, in law, not to have been victims of sexual assault merely because their attacker had a distorted, sexist understanding of sexuality.

Recent Complaint

Under old law, women who had been raped were expected to rush out and 'raise a great hue and cry', to tell people that they had been raped. It was thought that a 'good' woman would be so outraged by what happened that she would want people to know right away so that they could go after the attacker. If women waited before telling about the rape, they were suspected of having made up the story. They were asked why they hadn't said something before.

The importance of telling the story right away led to special rules called 'recent complaint' evidence. These rules allowed the prosecution to include as evidence a statement of the first person that the woman told about the rape. They also allowed a judge to make negative comments if the woman had not told someone right away.

These rules were 'abrogated', which means they were removed, in 1983 as a way of recognizing that many women find it very difficult to talk about their sexual assault right away.

This means that the crown counsel will probably be able to bring out the information that you told someone about the attack soon after it happened. However, the crown counsel will not be able to use what you said to that person, in order to show that your story was the same right from the beginning.

The defence may be able to raise the question of any delay in reporting the attack, and may also be allowed to bring in any evidence which shows that your story changed from the time you first told it.

Past Sexual History

Sexual offences are the only criminal offences where the sexual history of victims can be used by the accused to attack the credibility of the victim.

There are two main reasons which are used to justify questioning a sexual assault victim about her past sexual history. The first reason is that a woman's past sexual behaviour is used as a measurement of the kind of person she is, i.e. whether she is trustworthy, and likely to tell the truth in court. (A man's sexual behaviour is not generally seen as relevant to whether he will tell the truth.)

The second reason is that it is often believed that if women agreed to have sexual intercourse at one time, they may be more likely to agree at another time, for example, on the occasion being discussed at the trial.

For many years, rape victims who were giving their testimony in court were asked all about their past sexual activities. They were also asked about any other activities which the defence thought might show that they were 'loose' women, including such questions as "Is it true you used to model swimsuits?"

Many women found these questions embarrassing. They did not think that they had anything to do with being raped. This kind of questioning began to be the subject of more and more criticism.

Rape crisis centres pointed out that many women were not coming forward to report rapes because they did not want to go through the ordeal of having to talk about all the details of their personal lives on the witness stand. Many women's groups argued that the sexual history of a rape victim had no more to do with being raped than giving money away had to do with later being robbed.

In 1976 parliament put some restrictions on the kinds of questions that a rape victim could be asked about her past sexual history. These restrictions did not result in major changes. In 1983 the Criminal Code was changed again.

The new law still allows the victim to be asked questions about any past sexual history she may have with the accused. This will be difficult for a woman who was sexually assaulted by her husband or a male friend.

Now there are three remaining grounds which the defence can use to ask victims about their sexual activity with anyone other than the accused. These are:

1) where it contradicts something already mentioned by the victim when she gave her evidence in chief;

2) where it relates to the question of the identity of the accused;

3) where it is evidence about sexual activity which took place on the same occasion as the sexual assault.

A defence counsel is allowed to ask questions about your sexual history only on these grounds. S/he can only ask questions on the third ground, after s/he has given notice in writing to the judge of the intention to ask the questions, and of the kind of evidence that s/he expects to get from asking the questions.

If the judge is given this notice that the defence counsel wants to ask questions about your past sexual history, s/he will hold a hearing, called a voir dire. (See *The Trial*.) The public and the jury will not be allowed to be at the hearing. You may be asked to testify at the hearing, but you don't have to answer all of the questions.

The judge must allow the defence to ask only those questions which involve information which relates to a question about the facts. The information cannot be used to attack your general character. If the judge decides that the defence has a right to ask the questions the trial will continue. The defence counsel will ask you the questions again, and this time you must answer or you will risk imprisonment or a contempt of court charge.

Corroboration

Until 1976 a judge in a rape trial had to warn the jury that it was unsafe to convict on the basis of the victim's testimony by itself, i.e. uncorroborated testimony. Uncorroborated testimony is testimony which does not have any other evidence (witnesses, medical evidence, etc.) to back it up.

The only other cases where judges had to make this warning were those relating to the testimony of children who were too young to take the oath, and that of accomplices, i.e. others who helped the accused commit a crime. So rape victims, children and accomplices were seen as unreliable witnesses.

In 1976 this requirement was dropped from the Criminal Code. Some judges then decided that, while the Criminal Code no longer required them to make the warning, the common law (decisions by judges in earlier cases) required them to make it. So some judges continued to warn juries that women who complained about rape were unreliable.

In 1983, the Criminal Code was again changed. Now it says that judges in sexual offence cases must not tell the jury that it is not safe to convict in a case where there is little or no corroboration. This does not mean that judges and juries will necessarily convict the accused where there is no other evidence that helps to prove the case against the accused; it does mean that victims of sexual assault no longer have to suffer the added insult of being considered, in law, less reliable than other witnesses.

In 1988, Parliament also removed the requirement for corroboration of the testimony of children who do not give evidence under oath.

Similar Fact Evidence

The rules relating to similar fact evidence do not apply only to sexual assault cases, although this kind of evidence is used more frequently in these cases.

An example of the use of similar fact evidence would be where a man has sexually assaulted several women, in the same area, or by using the same methods, and he is charged with and put on trial for some or all of the offences at the same time. Crown counsel will then call the different women who were attacked to testify at the trial and will argue that their evidence should be admitted because the offences are similar in kind. The combined evidence of the women might provide more information than any one of the women by herself about the identity of the accused or his method of attack.

Similar fact evidence cannot be used to suggest only that the accused is someone who tends to commit crimes. To be admitted under the similar fact rule the evidence must be used to prove the identity of the accused, or that he intended to commit the crime, or that he used a certain system of operation.

The Preliminary Hearing

Where an accused has chosen to be tried in a higher court by a judge alone, or by a judge and jury, a preliminary hearing will be held. The purpose of the preliminary hearing is to find out whether there is enough evidence to put the accused on trial. It also gives the accused and his lawyer a preview of the evidence that will be brought against him during the trial. A Provincial Court judge will preside over the hearing and a written record, (called a transcript) will be taken of all that is said during the hearing.

The preliminary hearing will often not take place until three to six months after charges have been laid. If the accused is being held in custody, the hearing will usually take place sooner.

Where there are two or more men accused they do not have the right to separate preliminary hearings. Nor does an accused who is charged with more than one offence in relation to the same incident have the right to separate preliminary hearings for each offence.

The accused can decide to give up his right to a preliminary hearing, and the Attorney General can also decide to have the accused go straight to trial, although this is unusual.

If the accused runs away during the preliminary hearing the judge can decide that he has given up his right to be present and can carry on with the hearing. The judge can also issue a warrant for the accused's arrest and adjourn (postpone) the hearing until he is found. The accused's lawyer can continue to represent him if the judge decides to go on with the hearing. If the accused returns during the hearing he does not have the right to have the parts that he missed repeated. Where an accused absconds (runs away) the judge can 'draw adverse inference', which means that s/he can take the fact that the accused ran away into consideration.

Where the accused makes the request, the judge must make an order that the media cannot publish or broadcast the proceedings.

Moving The Hearing

Either crown counsel or the accused can apply to have a hearing or a trial moved to another place. This is called changing the venue. The reason for this kind of an application is that the crown counsel or accused thinks that it would be hard to have a fair trial in the community where the hearing or trial would normally take place. Women who have been sexually assaulted, and who live in small communities, will sometimes ask for a change of venue in order to have some protection against everyone in the community hearing about the sexual assault.

Until 1983, if the accused or the crown counsel in a sexual offence case applied for a change of venue, the judge would either have to grant the application or give the reasons for refusing to grant it. This has now been changed and, for the purposes of the change of venue, sexual offence cases are treated the same way as other cases. Now judges do not have to give their reasons for not making the order, which means that they are under less pressure to do so.

Excluding The Public

While there is a general rule that preliminary hearings and trials are open to the public, subsection 442(1) of the Criminal Code allows a judge to exclude all or some members of the public from the courtroom if s/he "is of the opinion that it is in the interest of public morals, the maintenance of order or the proper administration of justice".

Subsection 442(2) adds that where the accused is charged with a serious sexual offence, and the accused or the crown counsel ask that the public be excluded, the judge must either grant the request or give reasons why s/he is not granting the request.

This means that judges can decide to exclude the public, although in the majority of cases they will not. The judge will usually only grant the crown counsel's request to have the public excluded in cases where the victim is very young or where there is some other reason why it would be exceptionally difficult for her to testify in open court. While many women who have been sexually assaulted have refused to report the crime because they were afraid of testifying in open court, or have suffered a lot of trauma from giving their testimony, this fear is generally not seen by the judges as a good enough reason for closing the court.

Mentally Ill Accused

Where the judge decides from the evidence that there is reason to believe that an accused person is mentally ill s/he can require the accused to go for a medical examination. S/he can also detain the accused for psychiatric observation for up to sixty days.

If the judge has reason to doubt that the accused is sane enough to give his defence, s/he can hold a hearing to determine whether the accused is fit to conduct the preliminary hearing. If the judge then finds that the accused is not fit, s/he can order that the accused be kept in custody indefinitely. If the accused is found to be fit to give his defence the preliminary hearing will go ahead.

The Hearing

At the hearing the crown counsel does not have to prove that the accused is guilty, but must try to show that there is enough evidence to have the accused go on trial.

The crown counsel will also bring the physical evidence, i.e. the medical tests, the clothes that you were wearing at the time of the attack, and anything else that the police have collected which helps to show that the attack took place.

The crown counsel will sometimes make an opening statement to the judge to outline the case against the accused. S/he will then call the witnesses for the prosecution and will ask them to tell what they know about what happened. The crown counsel will not always call all of the witnesses for the preliminary hearing. Sometimes s/he will call only the witnesses who are most involved with the case.

Usually the doctor who examined you will be the first witness. Often the police will be called to testify after the doctor, but sometimes you will be called in to give your testimony next.

Each witness will first be examined (asked questions) by the crown counsel, and then will be cross-examined by the defence counsel.

After all the witnesses for the prosecution have finished their testimony and the crown counsel has submitted the evidence, the judge must ask the accused if he wishes to say anything, and must warn him that anything he does say will be recorded and can be used against him.

The accused can make a statement, but he does not have to take the oath. He has the right to, but does not have to, and does not usually give evidence or call witnesses at a preliminary hearing.

When the prosecution and defence have finished with all the evidence the judge will decide whether there is some evidence about each of the aspects of the offence which it is necessary to prove. If there is not enough evidence the accused will be discharged. If the judge finds there is enough evidence, the accused will be committed for trial, which means that he will be told that he will be put on trial.

Appeal From A Decision On A Preliminary Hearing

Although this does not happen often, a higher court can quash an order to stand trial which means that it can decide that the judge at the preliminary hearing was wrong to order the accused to stand trial. The grounds for quashing an order to stand trial are that the judge acted without jurisdiction (he did not have the right to make the decision) or that he made the order even when there was not any legal evidence against the accused.

Where a judge at a preliminary hearing has discharged the accused, the Attorney General can decide to put the accused on trial anyway. This is called a direct indictment and is very rarely used.

The Attorney General also has the power to stay (postpone) the proceedings at any time before an accused is found guilty or not guilty, but can restart them any time up until a year after they are stayed.

Transcripts

The accused has the right to buy copies of and read the transcripts (written record) of the preliminary hearing. The crown counsel can choose to give the accused's counsel copies of statements made by the witnesses, police notes, etc., but does not have to.

Many crown counsel will give witnesses the transcripts of their testimony at the preliminary hearing so that they can refresh their memory before the trial.

The Trial

The trial will usually take place between six months and one year after the preliminary hearing. If the accused is being detained in custody the waiting period may be shorter.

Before the trial you will be contacted to meet again with the crown counsel. The crown counsel for the trial will probably not be the same crown counsel that you dealt with for the preliminary hearing.

You will receive a subpoena or court notification which will say that you are required to appear to be a witness. The subpoena will be delivered to you personally by a sheriff and it will state the time and place of the trial. The subpoena will require you to come to the trial at the time given, and to stay until you have been excused.

If you are not meeting with the crown counsel on the morning of the trial, you can go directly to the waiting area outside the courtroom, and wait until you are called to testify.

The jury will have been selected before the trial begins. They will be waiting in a jury room separate from the main waiting area.

Pre-Trial Motions

Before the trial officially starts, and before the jury is called in, there will often be a series of motions to be discussed by the crown counsel, defence counsel, and the judge. These are called pre-trial motions.

In a pre-trial motion either the defence counsel or the crown counsel asks the judge for a particular procedure. These can include:

- a request for an adjournment to delay the trial;
- a motion for a change of venue; ⟩ see section on the
- a motion to exclude the public; ⟩ *Preliminary Hearing*
- a motion for a ban on publication; see section on *Media Coverage*

- a motion to allow the accused to inspect certain documents;
- a motion to exclude witnesses until they are called to testify;
- a motion to quash (throw out) or to change the indictment (charges), because it is incomplete, wrong, or there is a duplication of charges; a motion that the accused be tried separately on one or more of the charges;
- a motion to allow two or more accuseds to be tried separately.

The judge will listen to the arguments from both the defence counsel and the crown counsel and will make a decision on each of the motions.

Arraignment – The Accused Pleads

There is a general rule that the accused has a right to be and should be present during all of his trial. However, he can be removed from the courtroom for misconduct and the judge may then decide that the trial cannot continue. The judge can allow the accused to be absent for all or part of the trial, but this is unusual.

Where the accused absconds (runs away) during his trial he is assumed to have given up his right to be present, the judge can continue the trial is his absence, and the defence counsel can continue to act on the accused's behalf. The judge can also issue a warrant for his arrest and postpone the trial until either the accused is found or the judge decides to continue without him. If the accused does show up he does not have the right to have the parts of the trial that he missed repeated.

The accused will enter a plea in court. He is read the indictment (charges), and is asked to plead guilty or not guilty to each of the counts. The indictment will contain all the charges for which he was committed for trial as well as any charges which came from information which was disclosed during the preliminary hearing. This procedure is called arraignment.

The accused can ask the judge for more time to consider his plea or to prepare his defence, but the judge has no obligation to grant him more time. If the accused won't answer or refuses to plead the judge directs the clerk of the court to record a plea of not guilty.

The accused can decide to plead not guilty to the offence he is charged with, but guilty to a lesser offence. If the crown counsel agrees, this plea can be accepted, and the accused must be found not guilty of the offence with which he was originally charged. This will sometimes happen where the crown counsel and the defence counsel have discussed plea-bargaining.

Mentally Ill Accused

Where a judge has reason to believe that the accused is insane, s/he can decide to have a trial to determine whether he is fit to conduct his defence. If the accused is being tried by a judge and a jury, the jury will decide the issue of whether the accused is fit to be tried. If the accused is found fit to stand trial, the trial will continue. If he is found unfit to stand trial he will be detained in custody indefinitely, but if he is later found to be sane he can be tried on the charges.

Adjournments

Where an accused is being tried by a judge without a jury the judge can adjourn the case from time to time, and can delay giving a decision on points raised during the trial. Where an accused is being tried by a judge and jury, the trial can only be adjourned for periods during the day.

Except for the adjournment for lunch (which is usually for one and a half to two hours), and at the end of the day, you should stay around the area of the courtroom during the adjournments.

If you are giving your evidence or are under cross-examination and the court is adjourned, you must not talk with anyone about your testimony, and you should not talk with anyone except the crown counsel about the trial. Usually the judge will warn you about this, but even if s/he does not, you cannot talk about what is going on in the trial. If it is found that you have discussed your testimony the judge can declare a mistrial.

Motion For Mistrial

A motion for mistrial can be made by the defence where there is some reason to believe that there has been interference with the course of the trial which could have the effect of making a fair trial impossible or unlikely. A mistrial could be the result of members of the jury hearing about something which would be likely to make them prejudiced against the accused, or of witnesses sharing information about their testimony with each other or other people who are wandering in and out of the courtroom.

A judge does not have to grant a motion for mistrial unless s/he agrees that the interference is likely to result in unfairness to the accused. If the judge does grant a motion for mistrial, s/he can decide that there must be a new trial, in which case the witnesses would have to appear and give their evidence again.

The Case For The Crown

The trial will usually begin with the crown counsel giving an opening address outlining the case for the Crown. The crown counsel is not allowed to make any prejudicial comments nor to give any personal opinions about the guilt or innocence of the accused. S/he has a duty to bring out all the relevant facts and is not allowed to hide any facts which may hurt the Crown's case.

The crown counsel will then call the witnesses to give the evidence for the Crown. These witnesses will also have received subpoenas requiring them to appear to testify. The witnesses will normally be called in the order in which they became involved with the case, but often doctors and police will be called first so that these highly paid professionals do not have to spend a long time waiting. Some crown counsel will call the victim first.

The crown counsel must make sure that evidence is brought out about each of the necessary parts of the offences with which the accused is charged. This means that there must be proof of all of the elements of the crime, e.g. that the attacker and the accused are the same person, the date and place of the attack, that the attack was a sexual assault, that the victim did not consent to the attack, etc.

In some cases the accused will admit to parts of the offence. For example the accused might admit that he was the person involved in the situation, but say that the woman consented. If the accused makes such an admission, the crown counsel does not have to take the time to prove this element of the offence (known as the identity of the accused).

Where the accused does not admit identity, the crown counsel must prove it with respect to each issue to which it is relevant. This is usually done by asking witnesses giving their testimony to point to the person in the courtroom that they think is the attacker. Sometimes the defence counsel will ask the judge to allow the accused to sit with members of the audience to make sure that witnesses are not just pointing to the accused because he is sitting where the accused usually sits.

Aside from the police who were involved in your case, and the doctor who examined you, and, of course, you, the crown counsel may call any other witnesses who have information to give about the case. These may include the experts who examined your clothes after the police took them from you, or anyone who may have seen or heard part of the attack.

Voir Dire

Sometimes the crown counsel and defence counsel will disagree about what evidence can be introduced as part of the case for the Crown or for the defence. When this happens the judge will hold a voir dire.

A voir dire is a trial within a trial. Its purpose is to decide whether a particular piece of evidence is admissible (can be used in court).

In a trial with a judge and a jury the jury will be asked to leave the courtroom while the judge hears the evidence in question and the arguments of crown counsel and defence counsel. If the judge decides that the evidence is admissible, it will be repeated in front of the jury. If the evidence is found to be inadmissible it will not be repeated when the jury returns.

Where the trial is taking place before a judge alone, the judge will hear the evidence. If s/he decides that it is admissible the evidence is not repeated, but becomes part of the trial. If s/he decides that the evidence is inadmissible s/he must disregard it when making the decision about the guilt or innocence of the accused.

Where the defence counsel wants to ask questions about your past sexual history, a voir dire will be held (see section on *Special Rules of Evidence*).

Where the crown counsel wants to use a statement made by

the accused, a voir dire must also be held.

Cross-Examination By Defence Counsel

Each of the witnesses who has been called by the crown counsel will be cross-examined by the defence counsel. This means that after they have given the first part of their testimony and have answered the questions of the crown counsel, the defence will ask them more questions about what they have said.

Often the defence counsel will ask very detailed questions about the information that the witness has already given. If the witness' answers are not clear or are confused, the defence counsel may use this to try to show that the witness is not really clear about what happened. The defense counsel may try to use this to suggest that the witness is not telling the whole truth or has changed some parts of the story.

Cross-examination is not limited to the information the witness has already given but may explore any evidence which is relevant to the trial. If the crown counsel thinks that the defence counsel's questions are trying to bring out evidence which is not relevant to the trial, the crown counsel can object to the questions. The judge will then have to decide whether the evidence that the defence counsel is looking for is relevant. In these circumstances a voir dire may be held.

Defence counsel can cross-examine a witness on previous statements that the witness has made if they are different from what the witness is saying in her/his testimony. If a witness is being cross-examined about a verbal statement s/he made before, and doesn't admit making that statement, the defence counsel can introduce evidence to prove that s/he did make the statement. Defence counsel must, however, remind the witness of the circumstance in which the statement was allegedly (supposedly) made and give the witness a chance to admit making the statement before introducing proof that the statement was made.

After a witness has been cross-examined the crown counsel can ask the judge to re-examine the witness to bring out additional evidence.

When all the crown witnesses have finished with their testimony the Crown's case is closed. It can, in special circumstances, be re-opened with the permission of the judge.

Motion To Dismiss

After the Crown's case has been closed the defence counsel can make a motion asking the judge to dismiss the case on the grounds that one or more of the necessary elements of the case has not been proven.

If the judge agrees that there is not evidence on each of the essential parts of the case, and that a properly instructed jury could not reasonably convict on the basis of the Crown's evidence, s/he must dismiss the charges against the accused. If the judge finds that there is evidence on each of the elements s/he will then ask the accused whether or not he wishes to call evidence.

The Case For The Defence

Where the accused has decided to call witnesses the defence counsel can make an opening address to the jury. During the opening address s/he will outline the case for the defence, and will usually try to present the theory of the defence (an alternative explanation of the events in the case).

The defence can call any witnesses who have information about the case. These witnesses will be examined by the defence counsel and then cross-examined by the crown counsel.

The accused does not have to testify at any time during his trial. However, according to Section 12 of the *Canada Evidence Act*, if he does decide to testify he can be asked about any past criminal record, for any offences, he may have. If he denies having a criminal record the crown counsel can introduce evidence to prove that he does have a criminal record.

If the accused decides not to take the stand, the judge cannot make any negative comment about that decision to the jury or take it into consideration in deciding the guilt or innocence of the accused.

Available Defences

During the defence case the defence counsel will usually try to draw out information which backs up the theory of the defence. This theory will have to include a reason why the accused is not guilty. For almost all criminal offences there are certain allowable defences. In sexual offences cases these are usually that the identity of the accused is not proven, that the sexual assault (or other sexual offence) did not take place, or that the woman consented to the act.

There is, however, a particular defence which developed as a defence to a charge of rape, and which parliament has decided will now apply to all assaults, including sexual assaults. This defence is known as the 'defence of honest belief'. This defence means that where an accused brings evidence to show that he honestly believed that the victim was consenting, whether or not she was really consenting, then the accused cannot be convicted of the charge. This belief does not have to be a reasonable belief, although the judge must tell the jury to consider whether there were reasonable grounds for that belief. This means that even if you did not consent, if the jury or judge believe your attacker thought that you were consenting, he cannot be found guilty.

Closing Statements By Counsel

After both the Crown's case and the defence case are finished the crown counsel and defence counsel will make their closing statements. The defence counsel will usually make his/her statement first, unless s/he has not called any evidence, in which case s/he will make the last statement.

Both counsel will attempt to sum up the evidence which backs up their case and to present an argument as to why the accused should (in the case of crown counsel) or should not (in the case of defence counsel) be convicted.

If the accused is being tried by a judge without a jury, the judge will then make the decision on whether to find the accused guilty or not guilty.

The Judge's Charge To The Jury

Where the accused is being tried by a judge and a jury the judge will make a speech to the jury after the crown counsel and defence counsel have finished their statements.

The judge will usually go over the evidence which has been

brought out and give information on the importance of or problems with the evidence, and on the credibility of the witnesses. The judge can give his/her opinions on the evidence and on the credibility of the witnesses, but must tell the jury that they do not have to agree with the judge's views.

The judge must review all of the defence evidence and arguments and must, if the defence counsel has not done so, bring up any other defence which the accused can use. S/he must also tell the jury that, where an accused is charged with several offences relating to the same act, they can convict the accused on only one of the counts.

The judge must also instruct the jury on the questions of law which relate to the case. The judge must remind the jury that the prosecution has the burden of proving the case against the accused beyond a reasonable doubt, which means that if they have any reasonable doubts about any of the essential elements of the case, they must find the accused not guilty.

When the judge has finished the charge to the jury, the members of the jury will go off together to discuss their opinions on the case. Where the jury finds that it needs more clear instruction from the judge, the jury will be brought back into the court. The judge will then give the necessary information and/or can order that a particular piece of evidence be read to them.

A jury must decide on a verdict unanimously. This does not mean that they all have to agree about everything in the case, but that they must all reach an agreement about whether the accused should be found guilty or not guilty.

Although there is no time limit on coming to a decision, if the members of the jury are not able to come up with this agreement (this situation is called a hung jury), the judge can let the jurors go and order a re-trial with a new jury.

If the jury has reached a verdict, the judge, the accused, and counsel are called into the court. The foreperson of the jury is then asked to state the verdict on each of the counts.

The Verdict

As mentioned before, the crown counsel has to prove each of the essential elements of the offence beyond a reasonable doubt.

Neither the judge nor the jury is allowed to find the accused guilty of any offence if they think that there is a reasonable doubt about some or all of the elements. This is the case even where they might believe that the accused is guilty.

Sexual assaults are among the most difficult crimes to prove. The accused was convicted in just over one-half of those rape cases which went to trial. This means that in nearly one-half of the cases the accused was found not guilty. This is a much lower conviction rate than that for other violent crimes. We do not yet know whether the new sexual assault law will result in a higher conviction rate.

If the accused is found guilty, the judge will often order that he be held in custody until he is sentenced.

For many women who have testified about their sexual assaults a verdict of not guilty is extremely difficult. They often feel that it means that they were not believed and that the judge or jury didn't think that the sexual assault happened. They usually feel very hurt or very angry, or both.

To go through the very difficult experience of telling a roomful of strangers about a violent and humiliating experience, first, at a preliminary hearing, and then again at the trial, is extremely painful. To then have the accused found not guilty, and walk away free, when you have spent months or years going through the ordeal of criminal proceedings, is a bitter pill to swallow. Remembering that a verdict of not guilty is not your fault, and that you did the best you could, may be of very little help at this time.

Sentencing

There will often be a delay between the time someone is convicted and the date that is set for sentencing. Judges will usually request a pre-sentence report, which is a report on the background and circumstances of the offender written by a probation officer. Copies of the pre-sentence report will be given to the crown counsel and the defence counsel. The judge may also request that the offender be given a psychiatric assessment.

The Concept Of Sentencing

The general principles of sentencing are based on the ideas that prison serves as a deterrent (the threat of prison discourages people from committing crimes), and that prisons can help to reform the offender. Despite these ideas, many members of both the criminal justice system and the general public, as well as the offender, view a prison sentence as punishment. This view is held more strongly by those who are aware of the brutality of the Canadian prison system.

Sexual offenders are often held in protective custody. Otherwise they tend to be beaten up by the other prisoners who consider sexual offenders to be the lowest of the low.

There are few special programs for convicted sexual offenders. There are no methods which have been proven to be effective in reforming the men who commit violence against women and children. When they have served their sentences they are released into the community. After their time in prison they are likely to have even greater feelings of powerlessness, hostility, inadequacy, and anger against women than they had when they went in. Rapists very often rape again when they again have the opportunity.

Sentencing Considerations

Judges have a wide range of choices in sentencing. They are supposed to consider the age, background and circumstances of the offender as well as the type and circumstances of the crime. While the maximum sentences for offences are listed in the Criminal Code, (see *Appendix I*) very few crimes have minimum sentences.

The maximum sentences are viewed by judges as an indication of the seriousness of the offence rather than a suggestion of the sentence which should be imposed. For example, the maximum sentence for rape was life imprisonment. The average sentence was between three and one-half and four years, although the time served is much less as prisoners are often released on parole after having served only one-third of their sentence. It is too early to be able to detect a trend in sentences for the new sexual assaults offences.

While judges sometimes make comments about the protection of the public or the public disapproval of a particular kind of crime when they give their reasons for sentencing, sentences are generally made on an individual basis. This means that the judge's view of what kind of person the offender is, is a very important factor.

Victim Impact Statements

As mentioned before, the victim of the crime is treated as a witness. This has been a point of frustration for many women who have survived sexual violence and the court case which followed only to find that they never really got to tell what they thought and felt about what happened to them.

The criminal justice system has only just begun to recognize that the victim has a special interest in her case. While this has still not resulted in any special role for her in the trial, crown counsel in some provinces have begun to use victim impact statements at sentencing hearings.

A victim impact statement is an expression by the victim of the effect that the crime has had on her. Although the statements are not used during the trial, but only after the offender has been convicted, they provide a way for a survivor's feelings and concerns to be heard in the courtroom. It also gives the judge additional background information about the crime and its effect. The statement may be written by the survivor and then read, as a whole or in part, by the crown counsel at the sentencing hearing. Sometimes the crown counsel will ask the survivor to testify in person at the sentencing hearing about the effect the crime has had on her.

Some provinces automatically send out forms to victims asking for victim impact statement information. If you have not been asked to provide this information and you think that you would like to submit a victim impact statement, talk to the crown counsel. Write, in not more than a few pages, about the effect that the attack had on you, at the time it happened, and during the months following.

The crown has the right to decide whether to use a victim impact statement, but if you have asked to submit one, and the crown counsel says that s/he is unwilling to use it, ask why. If you are not satisfied with the reasons, ask to speak to a senior crown counsel or call a rape crisis/sexual assault centre.

Sentencing Procedure

An offender who has pleaded guilty or who has been found guilty, will be given a hearing. At this hearing information about the crime and the offender's character is presented to the judge by the offender or his lawyer.

Where an offender is pleading guilty, without going through a trial he will be read the charge and asked to plead. The crown counsel will then read out the facts, briefly describing what happened during the attack. The offender will then be asked whether he admits or denies these facts. If he denies some of them, the crown counsel may bring evidence and witnesses to try to prove these facts beyond a reasonably doubt.

Crown counsel can also address the court about the kind or length of sentence that s/he thinks would be suitable. The crown counsel can bring up the offender's past behaviour, including any criminal record he may have.

The offender or his lawyer can also make a statement during the sentencing hearing to try to persuade the judge that he should be given a lesser sentence. He can call witnesses to give information about his character, background and circumstances.

Sentencing Options

A judge can use any of the following sentences alone or in a combination with another:

Discharge: A discharge is not, technically, a sentence because an accused who is discharged is not considered to have been convicted. It is used when an accused has been found guilty, but the judge thinks that it would not be in his best interests to give him a criminal record or to impose a sentence. A discharge can also have conditions attached to it, such as a probation order. If the conditions are broken the judge can decide to revoke the discharge, convict the accused, and sentence him. A judge cannot order a discharge where an accused has been found guilty of a crime which carries a maximum sentence of fourteen years or life.

Probation: An offender can be put on probation for a period of time up to three years. During this time he must not commit any other offences and will have to report to a probation officer at regular intervals. There may also be other conditions in his probation order, such as no alcohol consumption, keeping a job, or not seeing the victim. If he breaks his probation order he can be charged with the offence of breach of a probation order. A judge can decide to suspend the sentence (which means to delay the passing of a sentence) and impose a probation order.

Fine: An offender who is convicted of an indictable offence which carries a maximum sentence of no more than five years can be ordered to pay a certain amount of money. If he does not pay within a set period of time, he can then be imprisoned. An offender who is convicted of a crime which carries a sentence of more than five years can be fined in addition to another sentence.

Compensation and Restitution: A judge can order an offender to return property or pay money to the victim of the crime. This is normally used only in offences of theft of or damage to property or in cases of libel.

Imprisonment: An offender can be sentenced to a term of imprisonment up to the maximum allowed for the offence in the Criminal Code (six months for summary offences, see *Appendix I* for indictable offences). If he is sentenced to two years or more he will serve the time in a federal penitentiary. Where an offender is given a sentence of not more than ninety days the judge can order that he serves the sentence intermittently (for example he spends weekends in prison and is on probation for the rest of the time).

Dangerous Offenders

Where an accused has been convicted of a number of serious sexual offences (usually at least three) the crown counsel, with the consent of the Attorney General, can apply to have him declared to be a Dangerous Offender.

There will be a hearing, without a jury, on the Dangerous Offender application. The crown counsel will be required to prove that

> the offender, by his conduct in any sexual matter including that involved in the commission of the offence for which he has been convicted, has shown a failure to control his sexual impulses and a likelihood of his causing injury, pain or other evil to other persons through failure in the future to control his sexual impulses. (*Criminal Code*, s. 688*(b)*).

At least two psychiatrists will give evidence at the hearing, one of which will be chosen by the crown counsel and the other by the defence counsel. Other witnesses, including the victims of the offender's past offences may be called.

If the offender is found to be a Dangerous Offender he will be held in prison, in preventative detention, for an indefinite period of time. This can mean a life sentence. If he is not found to be a Dangerous Offender he will be released after he has finished his sentence for the offence for which he was convicted.

Appeals

Although the decision of the facts by the jury cannot be changed, either the defence counsel or the crown counsel can appeal if they think that the judge made a decision which was not supported by the evidence or a mistake in applying the law. This appeal will usually be to the provincial Court of Appeal.

Either the crown counsel or the defence counsel can also appeal a sentence if they think it is lower or higher than it should be. Crown counsel will not normally appeal a sentence unless they think that it could be and should be substantially increased by the appeal court.

Appeal Procedure

Crown counsel or defence counsel must give notice that they are going to appeal within a certain time. The offender who has been sentenced to two years or more will not be sent to a federal penitentiary until the time limit for the appeal has passed. The appeal court can decide to let the offender out on bail until the appeal has been decided.

The offender does not have the right to be at the appeal where it is based only on a question of law, unless he does not have a lawyer to represent him.

The appeal court will review the transcripts of the trial, including the judges reasons for judgement. The appeal court can also ask the trial judge to provide a report on the case.

Normally the side that is making the appeal will argue that the judge made a wrong decision about admitting a piece of evidence or that the judge gave a wrong instruction to the jury.

The appeal court can hear new evidence on the case, including testimony by witnesses, but this is usually only done where it can be shown that the evidence was not available for the trial. It is most unlikely that you would be asked to testify again at an appeal. If the appeal court decides that the new evidence would have made the jury doubt whether the accused was guilty, a new trial will normally be ordered.

Where the court of appeal decides to allow the appeal because it finds that the verdict was not supported by the evidence, or that there was a wrong decision about a question of law, or there was some other miscarriage of justice, the conviction or acquittal will be set aside. The court may then order a new trial.

If a new trial is ordered and the Crown decides to continue with the case, you will be called to give your evidence again.

Criminal Injury Compensation

Most provinces in Canada have a fund to compensate victims of crime. These funds are based on the principle that society has a responsibility to provide money to those who have suffered as a result of someone else having committed a crime, because crimes are offences against society as a whole. The funds provide compensation to people who have suffered loss or injury as a result of certain types of crimes committed in the province. Most programs cover victims of many different Criminal Code offences, including sexual offences.

Criminal Injury Compensation provides an alternative to suing the person who has committed the crime, although you still have the right to sue your attacker, even if you get criminal injury compensation. If you have made an application and you do decide to sue, you must notify the Criminal Injury Compensation Board.

While it is not essential that you report the crime to the police, or that the attacker be found and convicted, the police and court records are seen as important considerations when your application is being reviewed. They help to show that a crime was actually committed.

Criminal Injury Compensation is less likely to provide compensation to victims who have not reported the crime. This is partly because they require some evidence that the crime took place, and because they want to encourage people to co-operate with police investigations. However, there is some understanding that victims of sexual assault are very reluctant to report to the police, and Criminal Injury Compensation staff may consider applications in cases which were not reported but where there is evidence which shows that the crime took place.

They do not require absolute proof of the crime, but they base their decision on the 'balance of probabilities'. This means they will review the information they receive and will provide compensation if they decide that it is probable that you were the victim of the crime, and that it is probable that you suffered the injuries you say you suffered. Awards have been made in cases where no charges were laid or where the accused was acquitted.

Don't wait until the courts have finished with your case, or until you have gathered all the necessary documents to apply. In some provinces you **must** apply for compensation within one year of the time that the crime took place. If you missed the one-year time limit because you were not told about Criminal Injury Compensation, or because of some other unique situation, you can apply and include a letter explaining why your application is late. They may decide to accept your application even though it is past the deadline. However, if at all possible, try to get your application in within one year.

Sometimes they will decide to wait until the preliminary hearing or trial is over before making a decision on your application. If they are not waiting for the criminal procedures the application will usually take two to six months, but it can, in some provinces, take a year or more.

The amount of the award depends on the kind and degree of your injury, wages lost and expenses incurred, the amount of pain and suffering, and your age and circumstances. Awards are paid in either a lump sum or in the form of regular payments. In sexual assault cases payment is almost always made in the form of a lump sum, unless a permanent disability is suffered, in which case a pension can be awarded.

Criminal Injury Compensation does not provide money for cash or things which were stolen from you, and some provinces do not pay for legal expenses.

To Apply For Criminal Injury Compensation

1. Phone for an application form. They will ask for your name and address and will send the form out to you. In some provinces they may take down the information over the phone.
2. Fill out the form as completely and clearly as you can. The form will ask you for information on the crime committed. If you have reported the offence the Criminal Injury people will be getting copies of the police and court records so you do not have to give all the details. Just describe basically what happened.

3. Consider claiming for things such as your lost wages or income, lost earning ability, and/or lost support for your dependants; damaged clothing; physiotherapy; counselling; the cost of replacing broken eyeglasses, teeth, dentures, hearing aids, etc.; your parents' or husband's lost wages for time off work; childcare expenses; medication or other medical expenses; and your pain and suffering. The Board can provide compensation in order to help a person to obtain work or to lessen a handicap resulting from the injury. While compensation may not be provided for all of these items, you may want to show the actual losses you have suffered as a result of the crime.

4. Where possible, send in receipts for all your expenses with the application. Any receipts which come after you have sent in the application should be collected and sent later.

5. Include, if possible, letters from your doctor, rape crisis centre counsellor, psychiatrist, therapist, physiotherapist or any other relevant person who can give information about the effect the sexual assault had on you. You can also write a note to explain the effect on you, yourself.

Applying for compensation is generally fairly straightforward. You do not need a lawyer to do it for you. If you do get a lawyer to help, some Boards will pay some of this expense, while others will not. If you have questions about compensation you can talk to the Criminal Injury Compensation office a rape crisis/sexual assault centre or a community law office.

When the Criminal Injury Compensation staff receive your application they will arrange to get copies of the police and medical reports.

Interim Payments

Some Criminal Injury Compensation Boards have the power to make interim payments where the person applying is, as a result of the crime, in financial need and it appears to the Board that it will probably award compensation. This means that if you need money before the final decision about the amount of your award is made, and you have no other reasonable source of funds, you can apply for some money during this period.

You do not need to make a special application for an interim payment. You can write on your application that you are in urgent need of funds, and request that the Board consider awarding you interim payments. Contact the Criminal Injury Compensation Board for further information.

Medical Information

In many provinces the Board will request the relevant medical information from your doctor. In some provinces you will be called in to be interviewed by a Criminal Injury Compensation Board doctor. This doctor will not usually give you a complete physical examination but will check out any injuries you may still have, and will ask you about any lasting effects of the attack. The doctor should allow you to bring someone with you into the interview.

Where The Decision Is Made By An Adjudicator

In some provinces, for example British Columbia, the decision on whether to award Criminal Injury Compensation is made by an adjudicator, who is a lawyer. If this is the procedure in your province you will be called for an appointment to meet with an investigator who will ask you about the offence and about your application. If you insist, the investigator should allow you to have someone with you during the interview. You may want to take notes of what is talked about during the interview, or to write down what was said immediately after the interview, so that you will have a record of what happened there.

The application, and the reports of the doctor and investigator will then be given to the adjudicator. When s/he has made the decision you will be sent a notice which will tell you what the adjudicator has decided, and the amount of the award that has been assessed.

Generally adjudicators say that they look at each case individually and have no hard and fast rules for making their decisions. Because of this it is hard to tell whether the amount of money they offer you is fair or not. You may want to check with a rape crisis/sexual assault centre to see if they have records of the amounts usually awarded in cases similar to yours.

If you are satisfied with the offer you must sign the form and send it back. A cheque will then be sent to you.

If You Do Not Agree With The Adjudicator's Decision

If you do not understand the decision or you don't think that the decision is fair, you can phone up the adjudicator and ask for an explanation. Or you can ask to meet with him/her. You can explain to the adjudicator why you don't think that the decision is fair. You can also talk about the decision with a rape crisis/sexual assault centre worker.

If you are not satisfied with the decision you can write to the Board and ask to have your application and the decision reviewed by an appeal committee. You can be at the appeal committee review. You can also get a friend, a rape crisis/sexual assault centre worker, or a lawyer to speak for you at the appeal committee if you wish. There is a further appeal available from a decision of this committee, with the consent of the appeal committee or of one commissioner of the Workers' Compensation Board.

Where A Hearing Is Held

In some provinces, for example Ontario, the person who has applied for Criminal Injury Compensation will be asked to attend a hearing, before one or more members of the Board. Although these hearings are generally public, they are closed to the public in sexual assault cases. This means, however, that you may not be able to have a rape crisis centre worker, or friend or family member with you. But you can have a lawyer to represent you, and if your application is successful, the Board will pay the reasonable and necessary costs of hiring a lawyer. The Board also has the power to prohibit publication of the evidence given at the hearing.

In Ontario, the Board is required to notify the offender of the hearing, and he is permitted to attend. However, where the offender is imprisoned or cannot be found he will not normally be able to attend the hearing.

In provinces where a hearing is held, you will not usually have a pre-hearing interview, although sometimes the Board will ask one of its investigators to make a report, and in that case, the investigator may want to talk with you.

The Board member or members may tell you their decision at the end of the hearing, or they may take more time to think about it and will let you know the result later.

If your application was heard by one Board member and you are not satisfied with the decision you can request a review of the decision. You must make this request within fifteen days. If you make this request, Board members other than the one who dealt with your application will hold a hearing and review the first decision. The decision of this review will be final unless new evidence later comes to light or the Board which made the review has made a mistake on a point of law.

If You Receive An Award

If your claim is settled but your physical or emotional injury flares up again, you can ask to have your application reopened.

WARNING: If you are receiving income assistance (welfare) at the time that you receive criminal injuries compensation money, you may find that your welfare office will ask you to sign a form which will turn over the compensation money to the Ministry. This procedure is not legal. If this happens, you should get legal advice.

The Ministry might deduct the compensation money you received from your welfare cheque. If you find this has happened, you have the right to appeal. When you appeal the money which has been deducted from your cheque will be returned to you until it is decided whether you will be able to keep the compensation money. The Ministry has the power to allow you to keep this money as compensation for the losses you suffered. An appeal tribunal might be persuaded to decide that the Ministry should use this power.

For more information on your rights, and on how to file an appeal, contact your local community law office, welfare rights group, or unemployment action centre.

Suing Your Attacker

You have the right to sue anyone who intentionally injures you, physically or emotionally. This includes the man who sexually assaulted you.

A suit is an action that is taken in a civil court (as opposed to a criminal court). A civil suit involves a private issue between two parties each of whom is represented by a lawyer of their choice. A criminal action is one taken by the state, on behalf of society as a whole against one or more people. A successful civil suit will result in the court ordering that the person who has harmed you pay you money in damages for the harm he has done to you.

Your attacker does not have to have been convicted in a criminal court in order for you to sue him. The decision in a civil court is 'on the balance of probabilities'. This means that your lawyer does not have to prove the facts 'beyond a reasonable doubt' (as in a criminal court) but s/he will have to show that the attack probably happened and you were probably injured by it.

Although you have the right to sue, a civil suit is a very long and expensive procedure. You will have to hire a lawyer. Because you are suing your attacker for money, a civil suit is only worthwhile if your attacker has or will have enough money to pay the damages. The present delays in the courts also mean that a civil suit could take two years or more to get to trial.

Sometimes you can find a lawyer who will act on your behalf on a contingency basis. This means that s/he would take a certain percentage of the damages if the suit were successful, and would only require that you pay the actual costs involved if the suit failed. To find out whether there are lawyers in your area who might take your case on this basis, you can contact a rape crisis centre or phone lawyers who are listed in the phone book. You can also phone Lawyer Referral, a service provided in most provinces by the Canadian Bar Association, to get the name of a lawyer who deals with personal injuries. The fee for the first half-hour consultation with one of these lawyers is usually between $10.00 and $20.00. Look under Lawyer Referral in the phone book.

Sexual Harassment at Work

Sexual harassment can range from upsetting or irritating comments, to pressure to submit to sexual advances or to serious sexual assaults. The expression 'sexual harassment' covers a wide range of abuse to which men submit their women co-workers or employees.

Sexual harassment can appear in the form of a 'joke', an 'invitation', coercion, or outright violence. The fact that it generally takes place among people who know each other is often used as an excuse to avoid taking it seriously. For the women who are sexually harassed, the workplace becomes a scene of repeated humiliation or a prison.

A common response to the issue of sexual harassment is the question "Well why don't the women just leave?" Many women don't leave because they are afraid they will not find a job elsewhere. Others don't leave because they know that what is going on is not their fault and they do not see why they should be the one to lose their job. Others are afraid that if they say anything, or leave, the harasser may try to make sure they do not have a good job reference.

If you have been sexually assaulted by a co-worker or employer you can take the steps outlined in this handbook. There may be some additional steps you can take.

Human Rights Complaint

The federal government and many provinces have Human Rights legislation to deal with sexual harassment. If you file a complaint with a human rights branch, they will normally have one of their staff investigate the complaint. They can then force your employer to change the work situation, and can sometimes get the employer to pay damages to you.

To make a complaint contact a Human Rights office.

Trade Union Protection

If you are a member of a trade union, notify your shop steward or your women's committee. Many trade unions are now developing policies and contract clauses on how to deal with sexual harassment. You may find other women in your union who have had similar experiences and who may be supportive.

If you are not a member of a trade union, you can report the sexual harassment to a personnel office or to your employer. Sometimes either or both will take steps to move you or your male co-worker to another department or job site. This clearly will not work if your employer is the one who is sexually harassing you.

Unfair Dismissal

If you protest that your employer is sexually harassing you or, that he has been informed of, and is doing nothing about, another employee sexually harassing you, and you are fired, you can sue for unfair dismissal. While a suit for unfair dismissal does not have to be very expensive, the amount of damages is not usually very high.

For advice on how to deal with sexual harassment in your workplace, you can contact a community law office, a rape crisis/sexual assault centre, or your local status of women office.

Appendix I

The Criminal Code—Sexual Offences

Section
139 *Consent Of Young Persons No Defence—Exceptions*

(1) Where an accused is charged with an offence under section 140 or 141 or subsection 146(1), 155(3) or 169(2) or is charged with an offence under section 246.1, 246.2 or 246.3 in respect of a complainant under the age of fourteen years, it is not a defence that the complainant consented to the activity that forms the subject-matter of the charge.

(2) Notwithstanding subsection (1), where an accused is charged with an offence under section 140 or 141, subsection 169(2) or section 246.1 in respect of a complainant who is twelve years of age or more but under the age of fourteen years, it is not a defence that the complainant consented to the activity that forms the subject-matter of the charge unless the accused

    (a) is twelve years of age or more but under the age of sixteen years;

    (b) is less than two years older than the complainant; and

    (c) is neither in a position of trust or authority towards the complainant nor is a person with whom the complainant is in a relationship of dependency.

(3) No person aged twelve or thirteen years shall be tried for an offence under section 140 or 141 or subsection 169(2) unless the person is in a position of trust or authority towards the complainant or is a person with whom the complainant is in a relationship of dependency.

(4) It is not a defence to a charge under section 140 or 141, subsection 155(3) or 169(2), or section 246.1, 246.2 or 246.3 that the accused believed that the complainant was fourteen years of age or more at the time the offence is alleged to have been committed unless the accused took all reasonable steps to ascertain the age of the complainant.

(5) It is not a defence to a charge under section 146, 154, 166, 167 or 168 or subsection 195(2) or (4) that the accused believed that the complainant was eighteen years of age or more at the time the offence is alleged to have been committed unless the accused took all reasonable steps to ascertain the age of the complainant.

140　*Sexual Interference With Persons Under Age Fourteen*
Every person who, for a sexual purpose, touches, directly or indirectly, with a part of the body or with an object, any part of the body of a person under the age of fourteen years is guilty of an indictable offence and is liable to imprisonment for a term not exceeding ten years or is guilty of an offence punishable on summary conviction.

141　*Invitation Of Persons Under Age Fourteen To Sexual Touching*
Every person who, for a sexual purpose, invites, counsels or incites a person under the age of fourteen years to touch, directly or indirectly, with a part of the body or with an object, the body of any person including the body of the person who so invites, counsels or incites and the body of the person under the age of fourteen years, is guilty of an indictable offence and is liable to imprisonment for a term not exceeding ten years or is guilty of an offence punishable on summary conviction.

146　*Sexual Exploitation Of Young Persons*
(1) Every person who is in a position of trust or authority towards a young person or is a person with whom the young person is in a relationship of dependency and who
　(a) for a sexual purpose, touches, directly or indirectly, with a part of the body or with an object, any part of the body of a young person, or
　(b) for a sexual purpose, invites, counsels or incites a young person to touch, directly or indirectly, with a part of the body or with an object, the body of any person, including the body of the person who so invites, counsels or incites and the body of the young person,
is guilty of an indictable offence and is liable to imprisonment for a term not exceeding five years or is guilty of an offence punishable on summary conviction.
(2) In this section, "young person" means a person fourteen years of age or more but under the age of eighteen years.

150　*Incest*
(1) Every one commits incest who, knowing that another person is by blood relationship his or her parent, child, brother, sister, grandparent or grandchild, as the case may be, has sexual intercourse with that person.
(2) Every one who commits incest is guilty of an indictable offence and is liable to imprisonment for fourteen years.
(3) No accused shall be determined by a court to be guilty of an offence under this section if the accused was under restraint, duress or fear of the person with whom the accused had the sexual intercourse at the time the sexual intercourse occurred.

(4) In this section, "brother" and "sister", respectively, include half-brother and half-sister.

154 *Anal Intercourse*
(1) Every person who engages in an act of anal intercourse is guilty of an indictable offence and is liable to imprisonment for a term not exceeding ten years or is guilty of an offence punishable on summary conviction.
(2) Subsection (1) does not apply to any act engaged in, in private between
    (a) husband and wife, or
    (b) any two persons, each of whom is eighteen years of age or more, both of whom consent to the act.
(3) For the purposes of subsection (2),
    (a) an act shall be deemed not to have been engaged in in private if it is engaged in in a public place or if more than two persons take part or are present; and
    (b) a person shall be deemed not to consent to an act
        (i) if the consent is extorted by force, threats or fear of bodily harm or is obtained by false and fraudulent misrepresentations as to the nature and quality of the act, or
        (ii) if the court is satisfied beyond a reasonable doubt that that person could not have consented to the act by reason of mental disability.

155 *Bestiality*
(1) Every person who commits bestiality is guilty of an indictable offence and is liable to imprisonment for a term not exceeding ten years or is guilty of an offence punishable by summary conviction.
(2) Every person who compels another to commit bestiality is guilty of an indictable offence and is liable to imprisonment for a term not exceeding ten years or is guilty of an offence punishable by summary conviction.
(3) Notwithstanding subsection (1), every person who commits bestiality in the presence of a person who is under the age of fourteen years or who incites a person under the age of fourteen years to commit bestiality is guilty of an indictable offence and is liable to imprisonment for a term not exceeding ten years or is guilty of an offence punishable on summary conviction.

166 *Parent Or Guardian Procuring Sexual Activity*
Every one who, being the parent or guardian of a person under the age of eighteen years who procures that person for the purpose of engaging in any sexual activity prohibited by this Act

with a person other than the parent or guardian is guilty of an indictable offence and is liable to imprisonment for a term not exceeding five years if the person in question is under the age of fourteen years or to imprisonment for a term not exceeding two years if the person in question is fourteen years of age or more but under the age of eighteen years.

167 *Householder Permitting Sexual Activity*
Every owner, occupier or manager of premises or other person who has control of premises or assists in the management or control of premises who knowingly permits a person under the age of eighteen years to resort to or to be in or on the premises for the purpose of engaging in any sexual activity prohibited by this Act is guilty of an indictable offence and is liable to imprisonment for a term not exceeding five years if the person in question is under the age of fourteen years or to imprisonment for a term not exceeding two years if the person in question is fourteen years of age or more but under the age of eighteen years.

168 *Corrupting Children*
(1) Every one who, in the home of a child, participates in adultery or sexual immorality or indulges in habitual drunkenness or any other form of vice, and thereby endangers the morals of the child or renders the home an unfit place for the child to be in, is guilty of an indictable offence and is liable to imprisonment for two years.
(2) Repealed
(3) For the purpose of this section, "child" means a person who is or appears to be under the age of eighteen years.
(4) No proceedings shall be commenced under subsection (1) without the consent of the Attorney General, unless they are instituted by or at the instance of a recognized society for the protection of children or by an officer of a juvenile court.

169 *Indecent Acts*
(1) Every one who willfully does an indecent act
    (a) in a public place in the presence of one or more persons, or
    (b) in any place, with intent thereby to insult or offend any person,
    is guilty of an offence punishable on summary conviction.
(2) Every person who, in any place, for a sexual purpose, exposes his or her genital organs to a person who is under the age of fourteen years is guilty of an offence punishable on summary conviction.

170 *Nudity*
  (1) Everyone who, without lawful excuse,
      (a) is nude in a public place, or
      (b) is nude and exposed to public view while on private property, whether or not the property is his own,
     is guilty of an offence punishable on summary conviction.
  (2) For the purposes of this section a person is nude who is so clad as to offend against public decency or order.
  (3) No proceedings shall be commenced under this section without the consent of the Attorney General.

173 *Trespassing At Night*
Every one who, without lawful excuse, the proof of which lies upon him, loiters or prowls at night upon the property of another person near a dwelling-house situated on that property is guilty of an offence punishable on summary conviction.

244 *Assault*
  (1) A person commits an assault when
      (a) without the consent of another person, he applies force intentionally to that other person, directly or indirectly;
      (b) he attempts or threatens, by an act or gesture, to apply force to another person, if he has, or causes that other person to believe upon reasonable grounds that he has, present ability to effect his purpose; or
      (c) while openly wearing or carrying a weapon or an imitation thereof, he accosts or impedes another person or begs.
  (2) This section applies to all forms of assault, including sexual assault, sexual assault with a weapon, threats to a third party or causing bodily harm and aggravated sexual assault.
  (3) For the purposes of this section, no consent is obtained where the complainant submits or does not resist by reason of
      (a) the application of force to the complainant or to a person other than the complainant;
      (b) threats or fear of the application of force to the complainant or to a person other than the complainant;
      (c) fraud; or
      (d) the exercise of authority.
  (4) Where an accused alleges that he believed that the complainant consented to the conduct that is the subject-matter of the charge, a judge, if satisfied that there is sufficient evidence and that, if believed by the jury, the evidence would constitute a defence, shall instruct the jury, when reviewing all the evidence relating to the determination of

the honesty of the accused's belief, to consider the presence
or absence of reasonable grounds for the belief.
*Subsection 244(4), above, is the defence often referred to as the
"defence of honest belief".

245   *Assault*
      Every one who commits an assault is guilty of
      (a) an indictable offence and is liable to imprisonment for five
           years; or
      (b) an offence punishable on summary conviction.

245.1 *Assault With A Weapon Or Causing Bodily Harm*
      (1) Every one who, in committing an assault,
           (a) carries, uses or threatens to use a weapon or an imita-
                tion thereof, or
           (b) causes bodily harm to the complainant,
           is guilty of an indictable offence and is liable to imprison-
           ment for ten years.
      (2) For the purposes of this section and sections 245.1 and
           246.2, "bodily harm" means any hurt or injury to the com-
           plainant that interferes with his or her health or comfort
           and that is more than merely transient or trifling in nature.

245.2 *Aggravated Assault*
      (1) Every one commits an aggravated assault who wounds,
           maims, disfigures or endangers the life of the complainant.
      (2) Every one who commits an aggravated assault is guilty of
           an indictable offence and is liable to imprisonment for
           fourteen years.

245.3 *Unlawfully Causing Bodily Harm*
      Every one who unlawfully causes bodily harm to any person is
      guilty of an indictable offence and is liable to imprisonment for
      ten years.

246.1 *Sexual Assault*
      (1) Every one who commits a sexual assault is guilty of
           (a) an indictable offence and is liable to imprisonment for
                ten years; or
           (b) an offence punishable on summary conviction.

246.2 *Sexual Assault With A Weapon, Threats To A Third Party Or
      Causing Bodily Harm*
      Every one who, in committing a sexual assault,
      (a) carries, uses or threatens to use a weapon or an imitation
           thereof,
      (b) threatens to cause bodily harm to a person other than the
           complainant,

(c) causes bodily harm to the complainant, or

(d) is a party to the offence with any other person,

is guilty of an indictable offence and is liable to imprisonment for fourteen years.

246.3 Aggravated Sexual Assault

(1) Every one commits an aggravated sexual assault who, in committing a sexual assault, wounds, maims, disfigures, or endangers the life of the complainant.

(2) Every one who commits an aggravated sexual assault is guilty of an indictable offence and is liable to imprisonment for life.

246.4 Corroboration Not Required

Where an accused is charged with an offence under section 140, 141, 146, 150, 154, 155, 166, 167, 168, 169, 195, 246.1, 246.2, or 246.3, no corroboration is required for a conviction and the judge shall not instruct the jury that it is unsafe to find the accused guilty in the absence of corroboration.

246.5 Rules Regarding Recent Complaint Abrogated

The rules relating to evidence of recent complaint in sexual assault cases are hereby abrogated with respect to offences under sections 140, 141, 146, 150 and 154, subsections 155(2) and (3), and sections 166, 167, 168, 169, 246.1, 246.2 and 246.3.

246.6 Evidence Concerning Sexual Activity

(1) In proceedings in respect of an offence under section 140, 141, 146, 150 or 154, subsection 155(2) or (3), or section 166, 167, 168, 169, 246.1, 246.2 or 246.3, no evidence shall be adduced by or on behalf of the accused concerning the sexual activity of the complainant with any person other than the accused unless

(a) it is evidence that rebuts evidence of the complainant's sexual activity or absence thereof that was previously adduced by the prosecution;

(b) it is evidence that rebuts evidence of the complainant's sexual activity tending to establish the identity of the person who had sexual contact with the complainant on the occasion set out in the charge; or

(c) it is evidence of sexual activity that took place on the same occasion as the sexual activity that forms the subject-matter of the charge, where that evidence relates to the consent that the accused alleges he believed was given by the complainant.

(2) No evidence is admissible under paragraph (1)(c) unless

    (a) reasonable notice in writing has been given to the prosecutor by or on behalf of the accused of his intention to adduce the evidence together with particulars of the evidence sought to be adduced; and

    (b) a copy of the notice has been filed with the clerk of the court.

(3) No evidence is admissible under subsection (1) unless the judge, magistrate or justice, after holding a hearing in which the jury and the members of the public are excluded and in which the complainant is not a compellable witness, is satisfied that the requirements of this section are met.

(4) The notice given under subsection (2) and the evidence taken, the information given or the representations made at a hearing referred to in subsection (3) shall not be published in any newspaper or broadcast.

(5) Every one who, without lawful excuse the proof of which lies upon him, contravenes subsection (4) is guilty of an offence punishable on summary conviction.

(6) In this section "newspaper" has the same meaning as in section 261.

246.7 *Reputation Evidence*

In proceedings in respect of an offence under section 140, 141, 146, 150 or 154, subsection 155(2) or (3) or section 166, 167, 168, 169, 246.1, 246.2 or 246.3, evidence of sexual reputation, whether general or specific, is not admissible for the purpose of challenging or supporting the credibility of the complainant.

246.8 *Spouse May Be Charged*

A husband or wife may be charged with an offence under section 246.1, 246.2 or 246.3 in respect of his or her spouse whether or not the spouses were living together at the time the activity that forms the subject matter of the charge occurred.

247 *Kidnapping—Forcible Confinement*

(1) Every one who kidnaps a person with intent

    (a) to cause him to be confined or imprisoned against his will,

    (b) to cause him to be unlawfully sent or transported out of Canada against his will, or

    (c) to hold him for ransom or to service against his will,

is guilty of an indictable offence and is liable to imprisonment for life.

(2) Every one who, without lawful authority, confines, imprisons or forcibly seizes another person is guilty of an indictable offence and is liable to imprisonment for a term not exceeding ten years.

(3) In proceedings under this section the fact that the person in relation to whom the offence is alleged to have been committed did not resist is not a defence unless the accused proves that the failure to resist was not caused by threats, duress, force or exhibition of force.

330 *Indecent Or Harassing Telephone Calls*

(1) Every one who, with intent to injure or alarm any person, conveys or causes or procures to be conveyed by letter, telegram, telephone, cable, radio, or otherwise, information that he knows is false is guilty of an indictable offence and is liable to imprisonment for two years.

(2) Every one who, with intent to alarm or annoy any person, makes any indecent telephone call to such person is guilty of an offence punishable on summary conviction.

(3) Every one who, without lawful excuse and with intent to harass any person, makes or causes to be made repeated telephone calls to such person is guilty of an offence punishable on summary conviction.

Appendix II

The Polygraph Test

Police will sometimes ask a victim of a crime to take a polygraph test (lie-detector test) to show that what she is saying is true. This procedure is not used in most cases. Many police detachments will ask a victim to take a polygraph test only when they do not believe that she is telling the truth. Sexual assault victims are asked to take the test more often than other victims of crime.

You do not have to take a polygram test. The rules of evidence do not allow the results of the test to be used in court. Although the courts are not convinced that the tests are reliable, some police continue to use them in their investigations. The following information may help you to decide whether you would agree to take the test if you were asked.

How The Polygraph Works

The polygraph machine, often called the lie detector, is an instrument which is designed to monitor certain physiological (bodily) reactions. The design and use of the machine is based on three assumptions:

1. lying is regularly accompanied by certain emotional states;
2. these emotional states are also regularly accompanied by certain physiological changes; and
3. that people cannot control these physiological changes.

The people who use the polygraph say that when someone has a guilty thought, when they know they are telling a lie, their body will react and this reaction can be recorded and measured.

The machine has four channels. Two channels record the breathing movements and changes in blood pressure of the person who is taking the test. The two other channels measure the electrical resistance of the skin which changes with varying sweat levels.

How The Polygraph Is Used

The person who the police want to test (called the 'subject') is asked to give her consent. If she is a juvenile, the police will have to obtain the consent of her parents.

If consent is given she will be interviewed by the person who will conduct the examination. The examiner will ask the person a wide variety of questions including questions about her background, medical history, family, etc. The examiner will observe the subject's physical/emotional responses to the questions and will form an opinion about whether she is telling the truth.

The examiner must also convince the subject that the polygraph works, that the machine can really tell when someone is lying.

While the examiner is supposed to be someone who is "unbiased", s/he is often a specially trained police officer or someone who may frequently do this work for the police, and is therefore likely to be influenced by the police opinion on the case.

The examiner will then put together a list of questions to ask the person during the actual test. Some of these questions will require that the person taking the test tells a lie. This will enable the examiner to monitor the reaction to a known lie.

Two of these tests are the card test and the control question test. In the card test the examiner asks the person to take a card and to answer "no" when the examiner names a card and asks if it is the same card as the person selected. In the control question test the examiner asks a question which s/he knows will provoke a guilty answer, such as "Have you ever stolen anything?" These tests are designed to measure the person's *general* guilty response and are used on the assumption that questions about a more recent wrongdoing will provoke a stronger guilty response.

There are other questions used by polygraph examiners to test guilty response to questions about the incident about which the police are concerned but these are used in situations where it is the accused who is being tested.

Problems With The Polygraph

There are both general problems with the polygraph test and other problems regarding its use on sexual assault victims.

Sometimes the tone or attitude of the examiner will affect a subject's response to the question. Generally the prior emotional state of the subject (usually very upset and tense in sexual assault cases) will also affect the findings of the test.

The machine can also be manipulated by subjects trying to alter their own psychological/physiological state. For example, using bio-feedback techniques, taking tranquilizers, putting anti- perspirant on the palms of the hands, self-hypnosis, or flexing muscles are all ways of distorting the physiological response to the questions.

Uncertainty, fear, stress, nervousness and thinking of other thoughts can also be interpreted by the machine as a guilty response. Some or all of these responses are common in victims of sexual assault.

The emotional anxiety experienced by sexual assault victims serves to make the results of a polygraph examination performed on a sexual assault victim probably less accurate than those performed on other subjects. As the accuracy of the polygraph is still not accepted by Canadian courts, its use by the police as an investigative tool on sexual assault victims is seen by rape crisis centres as questionable at best, and as a form of harassment at worst.

Suggested Reading

Bart, Pauline
  Stopping Rape: Successful Survival Strategies. New York: Pergamon Press, 1985.
Boyle, Christine L. M.
  Sexual Assault. Toronto: The Carswell Company Limited, 1984.
Brownmiller, Susan
  Against Our Will: Men, Women and Rape. New York: Simon & Schuster, 1975.
Butler, Sandra
  Conspiracy of Silence: The Trauma of Incest. San Francisco: Volcano Press, 1978.
Clark, Lorenne M.G. and Debra J. Lewis
  Rape: The Price of Coercive Sexuality. Toronto: Women's Press, 1977.
Delacoste, Frederique and Felice Newman, eds.
  Fight Back: Feminist Resistance to Male Violence. Minneapolis: Cleis Press, 1981.
Edwards, Susan
  Female Sexuality And The Law. Oxford: Martin Robertson, 1981.
Griffen, Susan
  Rape, The Power of Consciousness. San Francisco: Harper & Row, 1979.
Guberman, Connie and Margie Wolfe, eds.
  No Safe Place: Violence Against Women and Children. Toronto: Women's Press, 1985.
Harvey, Wendy and Anne Watson-Russell
  So You Have To Go To Court: A Child's Guide to Testifying as a Witness in Abuse Cases. Toronto: Butterworths, 1986.
Herman, Judith L.
  Father-Daughter Incest. Cambridge, Massachusetts: Harvard University Press, 1981.

Lederer, Laura, ed.
Take Back the Night: Women On Pornography. New York: Bantam Books, 1980.

Porteous, T. and N. Janitis
Let's Talk About Sexual Assault. Victoria Women's Sexual Assault Centre, 1984.

Porteous, T. et al.
Working With Survivors of Sexual Assault. Victoria Women's Sexual Assault Centre, 1986.

Rougeau, Christine et al.
A Guide for the Parents of Sexually Abused Children. Vancouver: Women Against Violence Against Women/Rape Crisis Centre, 1986.

Rush, Florence
The Best Kept Secret: Sexual Abuse of Children. Englewood Cliffs, New Jersey: Prentice-Hall, 1980.

Russell, Diana
The Politics Of Rape: The Victim's Perspective. New York: Stein & Day, 1975.

Russell, Diana
Rape in Marriage. New York: Macmillan Publishing Co., 1982.

Stanko, Elizabeth A.
Intimate Intrusions: Women's Experience of Male Violence. London: Routledge & Kegan Paul, 1985.

Sanford, Linda Tschirhart and Ann Fetter
In Defense Of Ourselves: A Rape Prevention Handbook for Women. Garden City: Doubleday/Dolphin, 1979.

Weibe, Kathy
Violence Against Immigrant Women and Children. Vancouver: Women Against Violence Against Women/Rape Crisis Centre, 1985.

Rape Crisis And Sexual Assault Centres

Many rape crisis and sexual assault centres provide 24-hour phone lines. They offer support, counselling, information and accompaniment. To find your nearest rape crisis/sexual assault centre, check the front of your phone book, or look in the phone book under "rape crisis," "sexual assault" or under "women."

If you don't have a rape crisis/sexual assault centre near you, you can phone a transition house/shelter for battered women to find out about support services in the area.

Your local crisis centre can tell you what resources are available in your community. Their number is in the front of the phone book.

Personal Record

It is generally very useful to keep track of dates and the names and contact numbers of the people you may deal with following a sexual assault. You may want to tear out or photocopy these pages and keep them in a safe place. Don't worry if you do not have all the information, or if not all of it is relevant, just use these pages as a list of things you might want to keep track of. You can also use the table of contents at the front of this book to make sure of all the steps involved.

Date and time of the sexual assault:_____

Where it occurred: _____

_____

Name of first person you told: _____

Date you contacted rape crisis/sexual assault centre:_____

Rape crisis centre phone number: _____

Name of rape crisis worker: _____

Names and phone numbers of any other support persons or counsellors: _____

_____

Medical Information

Date you saw a doctor: _____

Doctor's name: _____

Name of hospital: _____

Doctor's phone number: _____

Medication prescribed: _____

Date of follow-up visit to doctor: _____

Police Information

Date and time police were called: _____

OR date third party report was made: _____

Name(s) and badge number(s) of police who did the initial
investigation: _____

_____

Police phone number: _____

Date and place of interview with detective(s): _____

Name of detective(s): _____

_____

Detective(s) phone number: _____

Police file number: _____

The Attacker

Attacker's name: _____

Date the attacker was charged: _____

Charges laid: _____

_____

_____

Date of bail hearing: _____

Conditions of bail: _____

Charges to which attacker plead guilty: _____

_____

Criminal Injury Compensation (remember 1 year limit for applying)

Phone number of Criminal Injury Compensation: _____

Criminal Injury Compensation address: _____

_____

_____

_____

Date of application: _____

Date of interview/hearing: _____

Name of investigator/Board member: _____

Preliminary Hearing

Name of crown counsel: _____

Crown counsel's phone number: _____

Crown counsel's address: _____

Date and time for interview with crown counsel: _____

Date and time for preliminary hearing: _____

Court Address: _____

Courtroom number: _____

Name of Judge: _____

Charges on which accused was ordered to stand trial: _____

_____

The Trial

Name of crown counsel: _____

Crown counsel's phone number: _____

Crown counsel's address: _____

Date and time for interview with crown counsel: _____

Date and time for trial: _____

Address of court: _____

Courtroom number: _____

Name of trial judge: _____

Sentencing

Date of submitting victim impact statement: _____

Date of sentencing hearing: _____

Appeal

Date appeal filed: _____

Name of crown counsel: _____

Date of appeal: _____

PRESS GANG PUBLISHERS
is a feminist collective.
We publish fiction and non-fiction
that challenges traditional assumptions
about women in society.

For a free catalogue
of our books and posters write to
PRESS GANG PUBLISHERS,
603 Powell Street,
Vancouver, B.C.
V6A 1H2 Canada